Goddess Reclaimed

GODDESS
RECLAIMED:

13 Initiations to Unleash
Your Sacred Feminine Power

Syma Kharal

A transformational spiritual journey
for awakening women.

Toronto, Canada

Flourishing Goddess
Toronto, Ontario

The information shared in this book is meant to be inspirational. It is not a substitute for any psychological or medical treatment you may require from a licensed physician. The author of this book does not dispense medical advice or prescribe the use of any technique as a form of treatment for mental, emotional or physical problems. Any use of information in this book is at the reader's discretion and risk. Neither the author nor the publisher can be held responsible for any loss, claim, or damage arising out of the use, or misuse, of the suggestions made, or the failure to seek treatment or take medical advice.

Grateful acknowledgment is made to the Doreen Valiente Foundation for permission to reprint an excerpt from "Charge of The Goddess." © Copyright the Doreen Valiente Foundation.

Kharal, Syma.
Goddess Reclaimed: 13 Initiations to Unleash Your Sacred Feminine Power
1. Spirituality/Goddess. 2. Spirituality/Women. 3. New Age/Goddess.

First paperback edition October 2017

ISBN: 978-1-7750891-2-4
ebook ISBN: 978-1-7750891-3-1

FLOURISHING
GODDESS
FlourishingGoddess.com

TABLE OF CONTENTS

To the Goddess in every woman.

INTRODUCTION

I HAVE CALLED ON THE GODDESS
AND FOUND HER WITHIN MYSELF.
—MARION ZIMMER BRADLEY

You are the Goddess. Not a Goddess, but *the Goddess*. As a woman, you are the complete embodiment of the Sacred Feminine.

No matter how many times She and we have been oppressed throughout time, the Goddess still lives through you. She breathes through you. She creates through you. She destroys through you. She transforms through you. She rejoices through you. She grieves through you. She loves through you. She heals through you. She moves through you. She rises through you. She flourishes through you. Through and through, She is *all of you*.

While the Goddess already lives fully through you, beloved, you may yet be waiting to fully unleash Her power. If you have felt called to awaken your Goddess self, you have undoubtedly heard Her loving and urgent call to release patterns that block the direct and fullest experience of your Sacred Feminine gifts. Patterns where you might:

- Feel overwhelmed by the incessant noise and hyper-masculine pace of your life.

- Face constant outer blocks because you are not facing your inner, unhealed darkness.

- Trap yourself in disempowering situations by suppressing your raw, real emotions.

- Allow fears to hold you back from being and doing all that you are divinely meant to.

- Hold on to old pains and regrets that keep you stuck in the past.

- Let guilt and shame keep you from experiencing the love and joy you deserve.

- Settle for less out of fear of being unworthy or incapable of realizing your true dreams.

- Run yourself haggard as you struggle to follow plans and strive to meet goals.

- Compromise your own values and priorities to appease and accommodate others.

- Resent the "symptoms" of your feminine cycles and feel disconnected from nature's cycles.

- Block the flow of blessings and opportunities by over-giving and not receiving.

- Be afraid to hone and share your inner gifts and live fully on your Divine life purpose.

- Play small and refuse to take the lead in your life and be all that you came here to be.

Beloved sister, this is not who you are. And this is not honoring the Goddess within you. This is why She has called you back to Her, so that you may awaken Her gifts fully within yourself and ignite their power in every part of your life. Through the journey ahead, She stands ready to lovingly guide, inspire, and empower you so that you may:

- Gain clarity and peace by resting into the pure essence of your eternal spirit.

- Experience healing and wholeness by fully embracing all of yourself—light and dark.

- Transform what no longer serves you so that you can clear the way to create anew.

- Obliterate your fears and move forward as a fierce and powerful Warrioress.

- Heal the pain and keep only the lessons and wisdom from past experiences.

- Claim your sacred birthright to experience the love and ecstasy you deserve.

- Set your sights heavenwards as you align your intentions with your soul's greatest vision.

- Co-create your dreams with intuitive and inspired action, one joyful step at a time.

- Cultivate the courage to honor yourself and live with integrity and authenticity—no matter the cost.

- Harness and celebrate the Triple Goddess gifts of your womb, while reconnecting with the rhythms of the moon.

- Affirm your sacred self-worth and set healthy boundaries to magnetically attract the abundance of all the good you deserve.

- Shine boldly and brightly as you unapologetically own your spiritual and creative gifts, working miracles for yourself and others.

- Become the Sovereign Queen in your life and an inspiring example of feminine leadership in the world as you live fully from your Goddess-given power and invite fellow sisters to do the same.

These and many more are the gifts that await you on your path back to your Goddess self. That is what this thirteen-step sacred journey is, beloved: an invitation to consciously and progressively activate your Sacred Feminine powers through the Goddesses' inspiration and guided initiations.

As a woman, you do not actually require any formal initiation into your Goddess nature, for it is your nature. You were born initiated. All of your Sacred Feminine gifts are already inherent. When you embark on the guided initiations the Goddesses have channeled in each of their gateways ahead, know that you are not invoking a Divine force outside of yourself. Rather, you are consciously awakening the innate *shakti*—Sacred Feminine power—that already exists *inside of yourself.*

You are making the rightful choice to know and love yourself as the Goddess that you already are. You are owning your worthiness to reclaim your full feminine self, to bless and uplift not only your own life, but the lives of everyone you touch.

When you fully embrace your Goddess essence, you unleash the feminine force within that will heal and elevate your life. The more you honor your own Goddess nature, the more empowered you become in every part of your life and the more you inspire fellow women to step into their Divine power.

And we need this, beloved. The world is in dire need of us women reclaiming and rising individually and collectively in our Divine Feminine power.

WHY THE GODDESS WITHIN YOU IS NEEDED

We simply need to observe our world as it is and how it has been since the rise of patriarchy within the past 5000 years to see that in oppressing the Goddess, we have lost our balance. We have callously and selfishly dishonored Mother Earth for so long that now our very survival is at stake. We have favored consumption over circulation, competition over cooperation, and individual conquest over collective flourishing, bringing us to the critical state we now find ourselves in.

Just as Mother Earth has been degraded over the centuries, we women have been targeted, raped, marginalized, objectified, mutilated, abducted, tried, tortured, and even mass-executed during patriarchal reign. The gifts of the Goddess that were once celebrated and revered—our bodies, menstrual cycles, sexuality, fertility, intuition, compassion, creativity, resourcefulness, wisdom, knowledge, strength, wildness, wrath, magic, mysteries, and all sources and expressions of our feminine power—became threatening forces that needed to be tamed, owned, demonized, or eliminated by the "dark masculine," the unconscious shadow side of the Divine Masculine.

Even with the progress we have made in reclaiming our basic rights since the twentieth century, we have a long way to go to see all women and all people acquire fair and equal treatment, opportunity, and freedom. The shadow masculine is still trying with all its might to maintain its power and control through its outmoded and tyrannical structures. These systems have long served an elite few while subordinating and depriving the masses (women and men alike) and pillaging Mother Earth. Those benefiting from these structures continue to resist our collective efforts towards environmental responsibility, economic equity, and social justice.

The more the dark masculine fights to maintain its dominance, the more the Goddess is igniting Her Divine Feminine light within us. Every trigger we experience by the acts of unconscious leaders fuels the fires of rightful revolution within us. The Goddess cannot hold Herself back any longer, for She knows that She is needed now more than ever to save our planet and to save us.

While the twentieth century may have called for a more wrathful feminine approach to fighting for our rights (which, as you will learn, is perfectly Divine and sometimes called for), the Goddess is now calling on each of us to advocate for our rights by honoring our full feminine nature.

Where the brave generations of women before us—our mothers and grandmothers—often had to subdue the full spectrum of their femininity to be taken seriously in male-dominated social, political, and economic spheres, their very efforts have afforded us the ability to now confidently reveal our full feminine glory as we take back our power—individually and collectively.

One way the Goddess is enabling us to do this is by uniting us through increased transparency and connection provided by the internet and social media. Even among (for now) male-centric industries, She has inspired the creation of systems and tools that advance the feminine values of community, compassion, circulation, and collaboration.

This is a very exciting and long-overdue shift as we need the Divine Feminine and Masculine to cooperate and unite not only to thrive, but to survive.

We also need to work in consort with our fellow awakening men as they feel the Goddess rising within themselves and begin to move from their heads to their hearts. We need not continue to blame them, but rather inspire them to awaken through our own leadership and example. We need not fight them, but invite them into our collective healing as we resurrect our Sacred Feminine gifts and uphold values that serve us all. For together, we can create a new world, one in which both Goddess and God, women and men, are equally honored.

This collective healing depends on each one of us to reclaim our feminine power individually. Are you ready to reclaim yours, sister?

WHO ARE THE GODDESSES?

Whether you are new to or deeply immersed in your Goddess path, rest assured that the Goddesses are for all women (and all humans). They exist as deities that have been revered worldwide for tens of thousands of years. They exist as archetypes that permeate our collective consciousness and individual psyches. They exist as myths that inspire and guide us through our life milestones and challenges. And, as women especially, the Goddesses exist as inner aspects of our own Divine Feminine nature. The *Fusion Goddess* I co-created with my illustrator for the book cover represents only a few of these sacred aspects. How you connect with them is completely up to you, for they exist for you and through you, beloved.

Goddesses as Deities

As deities, the Goddesses have been venerated around the world from time immemorial and continue to be actively worshiped in indigenous, pagan, Hindu, and Buddhist societies. Scholars speculate that Goddess worship likely predates Neolithic earth-mother Goddess worship and may reach as far back as Paleolithic times.

As you will come to meet in the gateways ahead, the Goddesses are not just divinities of fertility, as archaeologists have historically maintained. Goddesses have domain over *all phases of creation*: emptiness, conception, life, death, and transformation. They exist in everything before, after, and in between. They radiate through the earth, moon, sun, stars, galaxies, and cosmos. They also rule the dark realms of the ether, void, and underworld. They are worshiped both for their celestial and physical powers as they pervade all realms.

The Goddesses are invoked for our very human desires for love, family, home, hearth, safety, health, success, and abundance as much as they are for our spiritual desires of creative expression, service, wisdom, and self-realization. Where male-dominated religions favor spiritual ascension over earthly desires (and even condemn these desires as sinful), the Goddesses honor all our desires as equally sacred for they themselves are both celestial and material.

Patriarchal religions see the pursuit of physical desires as an impediment to our souls entering heaven in the afterlife.

> *Goddesses have domain over all phases of creation: emptiness, conception, life, death, and transformation.*

Here is just one example of how desires for worldly good are denounced in the Bible:

> *Do not love the world or anything in the world. If anyone loves the world, love for the Father is not in them.* (1 John 2:15, (New International Version)).

The Goddesses, however, see embracing earthly life as a gateway to experiencing heaven right here, right now. They do not negate or shun our earthly desires because they are both the source of our desire and the blissful experience of its physical and spiritual fulfillment.

As mystic poet Rumi said, "There are a thousand ways to kneel and kiss the ground." So, too, do the Goddesses remind us that we can experience the Divine in all ways: through the sanctity of prayer and the ecstasy of lovemaking. All desires are Her domain. All experiences—of body and soul—are Her worship.

If you feel guided to connect with Goddesses as deities, know that no matter where they or you are from, the Goddesses are accessible to us all. They exist beyond the constructs of religion, culture, sex, and time. They exist through everything and everyone.

You may invoke them through prayer, honor them through ritual, behold their presence in nature, connect with them in meditation, and feel them in every moment, in each experience. However you feel guided to invite them in, every time you do, you are in essence opening yourself to having a direct, vibrational experience of the Great Goddess's energy and *shakti*, while offering yourself as a channel to receive Her infinite blessings.

Goddesses as Archetypes

Another way to connect with the Goddesses is to perceive them as archetypes. That is, as universal models, ideas, and symbols embedded in our collective unconscious. As archetypes, the Goddess takes on many forms:

She is the virginal, playful Maiden.

She is the Mother in the prime of Her sexual and creative years.

She is the Crone crowned into Her magic and wisdom at menopause.

She is the Triple Goddess, embodying all aspects of the Maiden-Mother-Crone and cycles of conception, life, and transformation.

She is the Creatress, Destructress, High Priestess, Huntress, Warrioress, Savioress, Temptress, Protectress, Enchantress, and Sorceress.

She is the Lover, Healer, Initiator, Transformer, Sustainer, and Nurturer.

Goddesses as Myths

Myths are one of our greatest tools for inspiration,

and the Goddesses have been the heroines of such epics since they were first recorded. No matter when or where they originate from, the myths of the Goddesses serve as profound catalysts for transformation and sources of empowerment for us women. This is because the truths they contain live beyond time and space and penetrate the inner knowings of our eternal souls.

According to renowned mythologist Joseph Campbell, myths serve four basic functions.[1] The first is on a metaphysical level, whereby their metaphors awaken a sense of awe within us that connects us deeply to the ultimate mystery itself. When we read the myths of the Goddesses, they pierce right through our feminine souls, eliciting a sense of resonance that is beyond the confines of conscious comprehension.

The second function myths serve according to Campbell is a cosmological one. To this end, myths are used to understand and explain natural phenomena that pervade our human experience. Goddess myths, in particular, have been used to explain the cycles of birth, life, death, transformation, resurrection, and renewal inherent in the earth and cosmos. Goddess tales are both inspired by and used to understand the phases of the moon, the dance of the stars, the rhythms of the ocean, the eruption of volcanoes, the creation of

---

1   Joseph Campbell with Bill Moyers, *The Power of Myth*, ed. Betty Sue Flowers (New York: Doubleday, 1998).

islands, the havoc of earthquakes, the dark depths of the sea, and the power of the elements.

The third function myths serve according to Campbell is sociological. Here, he suggests that myths were necessary and powerful tools used to preserve social order in societies that required conformity over individual will and freedom. As you will learn from *The Descent of Inanna* in Gateway 2—which happens to be one of the oldest recorded myths—one of the functions of Her tale was to warn ancient Sumerians of defying Divine law. For even Inanna, the Goddess of heaven and earth Herself, was not spared the consequences of doing so.

And yet Inanna's story simultaneously serves as an honoring of the risks we all must take if we are to venture beyond what is comfortable and embrace the unknown. Interestingly, many Goddess myths actually condone the defiance of conformity and celebrate the free will of the individual (especially women), which is perhaps one of the very reasons the rise of patriarchal order did its best to suppress or pervert them.

Goddess tales help us understand the phases of the moon, the dance of the stars, the rhythms of the ocean, the eruption of volcanoes, the creation of islands, the havoc of earthquakes, the dark depths of the sea, and the power of the elements.

The fourth and final purpose of myths according to Campbell is pedagogical, in which they serve as sources of inspiration to guide us through life challenges. In this sense, Goddess myths are deeply effective as they support us women in particular through the sacred milestones of our lives. As an example, the myths across various cultures around the Triple Goddess (the Maiden, Mother, and Crone) serve to support and empower us as we are initiated into menarche, motherhood, and menopause.

As you enter each gateway ahead, you will find that some Goddesses share their myths in-depth, while others focus more on the essence of their origin and attributes. I honored each Goddess in whichever way She wished to share Herself through me with you, beloved. And I trust that as you connect with either the details or spirit of each Goddess's myth, they will serve you not only on all the levels Campbell proposed, but on levels much deeper and far beyond.

Because the Goddesses are already a part of you, in learning about them you are in truth just remembering your own nature, which is also the next level in which you can connect with them.

Goddesses as Innate Feminine Powers

The last and most personal way to connect with the Goddesses is to know, feel, and experience them as Sacred Feminine aspects of your own self. The multi-faceted nature of the Goddesses represents the many dimensions of your own womanly nature.

As you will learn in Gateway 3, for example, Pele is the fiery power of your feminine wrath and your ability to create, destroy, and transform. In Gateway 6, Aphrodite embodies your sexuality, sensuality, radiance, joy, vulnerability, and capacity to love and be loved. Lilith in Gateway 9 reinforces your integrity, authenticity, and independence. Brigid in Gateway 12 is the source of your intuitive and creative gifts.

Each Goddess is an expression of your human and Divine qualities. Her attributes are your own inner gifts. When you connect with the Goddesses in this way, you embrace the full range of their nature, and therefore your own. You activate dormant forces embedded in your blood and bones. You awaken ancient feminine wisdom resting deep within your soul. You ignite their radiance through your heart. You unleash their magic fully in your life.

On the journey ahead and through your life, you are the only one to decide how you wish to connect with the Goddesses. When you read the inspiration and partake in the initiations in the gateways ahead, know that no matter how they expressed themselves through me, the Goddesses welcome you to perceive and experience them in whatever way most resonates with and serves you.

There may be some Goddesses you instantly resonate with and want to further awaken. And there may be some you feel resistance towards as they will stretch you beyond your comfort zone. Give them all a chance, beloved. For they represent a part of you that is your Divine right to love and own.

Do know that there is no right or wrong way to connect with them. For, above all, the Goddesses represent and respect your own feminine intuition. Simply trust and honor it.

MY JOURNEY TO THE GODDESS

As the daughter of very traditional and religious Pakistani Muslim immigrants with a childhood marked by every form of abuse, my path to the Goddess was not a likely one.

I was blessed to be born in Toronto, Canada where I spent the early part of my childhood as a shy, sensitive, and imaginative little girl. My parents strongly encouraged my intelligence and creativity, and even affectionately entertained my whimsical world and magical fairy friends.

The bright side of my family life, however, was overshadowed by physical, verbal, and emotional abuse inflicted primarily by my father towards my mother, my sisters, and me. While my mother would also hit us, it was my father's volatile nature that constantly petrified me.

When I was seven, my parents decided to resettle

us in Pakistan, where we lived for the next four years. From the age of seven to eleven, I was sexually molested by eleven men under my parents' care. They ranged from house guests and helpers to relatives and even a *molvi* (a Muslim priest).

When my father got word of the first man (a neighbor's guard) who assaulted me, he responded by locking me in a room and beating me with a thick wooden log. I naturally concluded that what the men did was my fault and that I would be punished rather than protected by my father.

In time, I managed to summon the courage to tell my mother about the houseworkers who consistently abused me.[2] She responded by either taking their word over mine and kept them, or fired them temporarily. After my failed attempts to get rid of them, the men became emboldened. They threatened to murder my family in their sleep if I ever reported their assaults again and didn't comply with their demands. I spent the nights of those years fearing for my physical and spiritual safety as I expected I would be going to hell for being a bad, sinful girl.

We returned to Canada when I was almost twelve and I immediately shut out the dark memories of those years from my conscious awareness. But they found a way to surface through symptoms of post-traumatic

---

2   In Pakistan it is common to have hired help.

stress disorder (PTSD). As a teenager, I developed severe depression, self-loathing, anxiety, nightmares, triggers, and hyper-vigilance. I would cut myself and write in my diary with my own blood. I wanted to die and only refrained from taking my life for fear of going to hell and devastating my family.

By Divine grace, when my teachers observed the signs of PTSD, they enlisted me in counseling with the school social worker and on-site psychologist. I was blessed to receive therapy for the entirety of my high school years, during which I also delved into spiritual healing practices. The combination of the therapies helped me process my traumas and become a functional, healthy, and even happy young woman by the time I graduated.

Nevertheless, due to my parents' increasing strictness and religiousness, even in Canada, I continued to fight many battles to have what are considered basic rights for women in the West. While these hard-won accomplishments awakened my Warrior Goddess power, by the time I reached my mid-twenties, the Goddesses were ready to initiate me into my *full* feminine power.

They did so by descending me into a second, severe wave of depression. It was during this dark night of the soul that I was more deeply graced with the love and light of the Goddesses. The gift from this depression was that it invited me to face the unconscious, energetic, and even karmic roots behind the painful patterns that kept resurfacing in my life *in a Sacred Feminine way.*

The therapy during my adolescent years was necessary and invaluable to my recovery from PTSD, so much so that I obtained an honors degree in psychology and a certificate in counseling from the University of Toronto because of it. But the depression of my twenties was initiating me into an even deeper level of healing and wholeness. It was offering itself as a catalyst for me to recover and reclaim my Goddess self.

I realized that in spite of the very helpful healing work I had done in the past, that as a woman, the modern Western and even ancient spiritual techniques that served me before fell short of fully addressing my physical, mental, emotional, energetic, and spiritual nature as a woman. And how could they, for they were created by (and generally made for) men?

For example, while the Vedic and Buddhist meditation techniques I learned helped me observe my pain from a place of detachment, they guided me away from delving into my pain—to feel and own it. The Goddesses, however, showed me that as a woman, it was vital for me to fully feel my pain before I could heal it.

Another revelation was when I realized that instead of just talking about my feelings to process them, that unleashing them through physical movement, sound, or sacred ceremony profoundly elevated my experience of release.

And so it wasn't until I re-discovered the buried ancient mysteries and wisdom teachings of the Goddesses that I was able to truly heal and flourish on every level as a woman. At first, embracing the Goddesses of the underworld led me to uncover the deep-seated lack of self-love, self-worth, and self-value that was mirrored back to me in my outer patterns.

Connecting with the High Priestess Goddesses then revealed that my wounds didn't just stem from my childhood—they were rooted in traumas from past lives and required healing at this level. I continued my journey with many other Goddesses as they showed up at the completion of each test, lesson, and initiation.

By fully committing to this transformational Sacred Feminine path, the Goddesses didn't just help me mend all that was broken. They inspired me to reclaim my Divine worth and live from my sacred truth as an expression and embodiment of the Goddess Herself.

As I continued to hone and own the countless Sacred Feminine gifts of my Goddess nature, my life transformed in miraculous ways as the Goddesses helped me:

- Gain the self-love I needed to release a toxic romantic entanglement.

- Fall in love with myself, my body, and my life.

- Manifest my beloved soulmate and husband, Eric, who makes me feel like a Goddess everyday, in every way.

- Release shame, guilt, and fear around my sexuality so that I could allow and expect myself to be ravished and cherished.

- Heal and evolve my relationship with my parents and set healthy boundaries (and in all my relationships) to ensure mutual respect.

- Stand up to and eventually leave abusive bosses and an unfulfilling corporate career.

- Use the lessons, gifts, and qualifications I gained on my personal journey to follow my calling as Sacred Feminine coach, healer, yoga teacher, speaker, and author.

- End patterns of financial struggle and embrace abundance and success—from *doing what I love.*

- Create a lifestyle that grants me the freedom to live and work wherever I want.

- Fulfill my dream of traveling the world and visiting sacred Goddess sites.

- Be blessed with the privilege and honor of serving fellow sisters all over the world to reclaim their Divine Feminine power and help them flourish in every way, into the Goddesses they truly are.

When I consider how I felt during most of my early years, I would not have expected to be alive today, much less fathom living such a blessed and flourishing life. I know that to come as far as I have is nothing short of miraculous. This doesn't mean that my life is perfect or that I always feel blissful, for life constantly brings me new levels of initiation—invitations to grow through inner and outer challenges. What is different now, however, is that I am able to embrace the cycles of life and my own feminine nature with the grace, wisdom, and power of the Goddesses that I have awakened along my journey.

And because I was saved by the love of and exalted by the power of the Goddess to get here, it is my deepest honor and joy to share the profound teachings and tools that have transformed my life with you, beloved. I know that if the inner and outer miracles I have experienced are possible for me—for someone who had no hope or strength for so long—then they are possible for *anyone*.

I believe that it is the right of every human being to know their Divine nature. I believe that this is why we have come here: to remember and be who we truly are. And every trial

> *It is the right of every woman—no matter what her culture or conditions—to resurrect and live from her full Goddess glory.*

and triumph we experience on our human journeys is an invitation to further uncover and express our sacred selves.

I also know that it is the right of every woman—no matter what her culture or conditions—to resurrect and live from her full Goddess glory. With the path that I have walked to recover mine, it is my sacred mission to do everything in my power to help you reclaim yours, sister.

Let us begin.

How to Use This Book

The Reveal of the Goddesses

This book is my humble, heart-filled offering to you and the Goddess, beloved. Its seed was conceived within me many years ago. But it required further personal initiations and the experience of serving thousands of women all over the world before I could share the insights, teachings, and tools that waited to be birthed.

Writing this book has been a beautiful Sacred Feminine journey for me personally. I had known that there would be thirteen Goddess initiations that would come through. Thirteen is a sacred number of the Goddess, as it corresponds to Her annual moon and menstrual cycles. I already offered a thirteen-session

Goddess mentoring program, so I had an intuitive sense of the journey they wanted me to take you on.

Yet, for this book, They revealed Themselves to me in Their own way and time. Last fall, Eric and I visited his magical homelands of Scotland and England to celebrate our anniversary. There, I had the blessing of visiting Glastonbury, which is known to be the realm of Avalon. Avalon is the land of many Celtic Goddesses, as well as the land of Mary Magdalene and Mother Mary. At Their sacred site of the Chalice Well, I performed ceremonies to honor the Goddesses and then offered myself as a clear vessel for their rising and flourishing.

As I sat in this receptive and reverent state, They showed me the book that I was to write and began lining up before me. The first few Goddesses were very clear, as I could instantly see and feel Them. The second half were there but veiled, and They assured me They would unveil Themselves in Divine timing. But Their directive was clear: the best way I could be of highest service to Them and fellow sisters was to begin to write this book. It was time.

Since the Well is a sacred site for the Celtic Goddess Brigid, who, as you will learn, ignites the Divine creative spark (especially for healers and writers), I started channeling the Goddesses' messages in my journal right then and there. Throughout the winter, I continued to incubate and nurture the messages they were sharing as they revealed the thirteen-step journey in their mysterious but perfect way.

After blessed Ostara (spring equinox), I started writing the first chapters. By the time we visited Egypt for my birthday in May, the rest of the Goddesses fully revealed Themselves, and it was crystal clear who the final initiatory Goddess needed to be and why She waited until I visited Her in Her ancient temples to appear.

Interestingly, but not surprisingly, I found that whichever Goddess's gateway I was writing about, my clients would also be struggling with the exact challenges that specific Goddess helps with during that time. And they loved receiving Her support and activating Her gifts, which were extra potent as I myself was immersed in Her energy.

In addition to the years of learning, experiencing, and teaching about the Goddesses, I wrote every word in this book after first honoring each Goddess in Her own way, through the same rituals that I teach in my High Priestess Training. By immersing myself in these sacred practices during the writing process, each gateway became a deeply embodied adventure with the Goddesses. And I hope that as you read each word, you can feel the beautiful, potent, and loving energy of these experiences transmitted through them.

Writing this book has been just as much a journey for me as I hope it will be for you. The Goddesses have taken me through all the initiations you will go through, and I hope you find them to be as powerful and transformative as I have, and yet in your own unique way. The journey goes through what I have experienced in my life and developed in my practice to be a gradual, step-by-step process to inner transformation. It is based on the ancient mysteries and phases of inner alchemy shared in a Sacred Feminine way to honor our womanly needs.

The Goddesses you will meet are from diverse cultures and backgrounds as They are like us all and for us all. I know that They will support you fully with Their infinite love as you embark on this sacred journey.

Embracing One Gateway at a Time

Because of the progressive nature of the journey, the best way to embark on this path (at least for the first time) is to go through one gateway at a time, in the order in which they are set forth. Based on my experience as a coach and healer, I have found that the feminine path to healing and empowerment involves first creating sacred space, then delving into the darkness, and then healing and clearing what no longer serves us while keeping only our soul lessons as we move forward.

Once our darkness has been brought into the light and felt, honored, and healed are we then ready to create anew from a clear and fertile foundation. And thus, the Goddesses you meet after the "darker" Goddesses (who aren't afraid of doing the uncomfortable but essential inner work), you will be ready to embrace self-love, set new standards and dreams, and gain clarity on your next steps.

As you continue with the last few Goddesses, you will gain the courage to be true to yourself as you reclaim even more of your Divine gifts. By the end, the Goddesses will help you unleash your Sacred Feminine power fully and boldly in your life and in the world.

EMBARKING ON EACH GATEWAY

In every gateway, you will first learn about each Goddess's nature and origin. You will explore how Her experiences and gifts might apply to your own life.

Next, you will be invited to embark on the initiation each Goddess has to offer in order for you to awaken Her power within you. The initiations offer a Sacred Feminine way to consciously activate, embody, and integrate your connection with the specific Goddess of each gateway.

These initiations are very much like the personalized healing journeys I lead in my client sessions and Goddess circles. Some are guided meditations, some are movement experiences, and some are journaling sessions. I honored whatever practice I felt each Goddess wished to share with you through me.

Every initiation ahead was channeled directly from each Goddess, where I delved into a meditative state as I wrote and through which I could feel Her working directly with and through you in powerful ways. As such, I invite you to treat each initiation as a sacred ceremony with yourself. Honor this sacred time by turning each session into a ritual, for rituals serve as a bridge from the mundane into the Divine. They transport you from the chaos of the outer world into the magic of the inner realms.

PRE-INITIATION PREPARATION

To create sacred and embodied rituals for each initiation, I have shared preparatory suggestions which you may wish to read in advance (a day or two before) each gateway. This will give you time to gather the suggested items if you choose to use them.

If you wish to know or gather the items before starting the journey, here is a list that covers the non-perishable items (some rituals call for fresh flowers, fruits, etc.) in all the initiations:

- Journal and pen

- White tealight candles (thirteen if you wish to use one for each ritual)

- Colored tealight candles (three or four each of): blue, orange, red, black, pink, green, yellow, and gold

- Incense (thirteen sticks if you wish to use one for each initiation)

- Ocean or spring water

- Bowl

- Coconut or olive oil

- Rose essential oil

- Sea salt

- Rose quartz crystal (smooth and tumbled)

- A sensual nightgown

- Any or all of: seashells, sand, pearls, moonstone, and/or turquoise crystals

- White or blue long skirt or sarong

- Jewelry: silver, seashell, pearl, moonstone, turquoise, gold, and a tiara/crown/headpiece

- Rattle (you can make one by putting rice in a sealed container)

- Makeup: Black eyeliner, mascara, red lipstick, and anything else you prefer

- A luxurious perfume or essential oil of your choice

- A decorative cloth to place on your chair

- A queenly/fancy long dress

Remember, the suggestions are just that: suggestions. You can bypass or modify them as your own intuition guides you to. For example, you can simply use white candles instead of colored ones if that's easier or your preference. This is *your journey*. Pursue it in whatever way best serves you.

That said, there are some essential steps to follow for your own well-being, comfort, and safety. Please ensure you:

- Discuss any conditions or contraindications you may have with a licensed medical professional as the information and exercises shared in this book are not meant to be used to replace or interfere with any psychological or medical care you may need.

- Have complete privacy when you practice each initiation.

- Place any fire-based tools (candles, incense, smudging wands, etc.) safely and burn them out completely after each session.

Here are some additional suggestions for honoring each initiation and your journey ahead:

- Create a sacred space. It would be ideal to have a dedicated sacred space to come to for your initiations. Clean out a nook or corner in your bedroom or home where you will have the privacy required, and consecrate it as your sanctuary. Adorn it as you feel guided. Gifts from Gaia (crystals, flowers, essential oils, incense) always honor the Goddess within. You can also place the image of each Goddess on your altar by opening your book to Her page.

- Buy a new journal and pen especially for this journey.

- Keep a shawl, cushion, meditation mat, or any other items at your altar to make you feel more supported and comfortable.

- Advise those you live with of your need for privacy, and even place a "Quiet please" or "Do not Disturb" sign on your door, and lock your door if possible.

- Turn off any gadgets and notifications that could interrupt your sacred time.

- Center yourself before each ritual with some deep breathing or a brief meditation.

- Set a heart-intention for your initiation based on the Goddess you are working with.

- Read each initiation fully first to familiarize yourself with the journey. When ready, read it again in sections as you practice each part.

Bonus Gift: Free Goddess Sige Initiation MP3!

To support you in getting centered during your journey, it is my joy to offer you a heart-gift, beloved: a free MP3 recording of the first initiation, "Entering the Void" with initiatory Goddess Sige. You may download the MP3 at: **FlourishingGoddess.com/sigemp3**.

Post-Initiation Self-Care:

As each initiation works on many levels and holds the potential to affect powerful shifts, it is essential to ground yourself afterward.

While I share specific self-care suggestions after each initiation, here are some practices that will help you best assimilate and integrate the effects every time:

- Ground yourself by wiggling your toes, imagining roots growing from the base of your spine and soles of your feet into Mother Earth, walking in nature, or touching your plants or pets.

- Write your experiences and reflections in your journal.

- Drink plenty of water (add a fresh lemon!) to support the clearing effects of each initiation.

- Take a cleansing bath with sea salts and essential oils.

- Nourish yourself with a healthy meal.

- Do something light-hearted and uplifting, especially after any initiations that feel intense.

- Shield your energy by visualizing a golden sphere of light all around you.

After each initiation, the Goddesses also shared Their own sacred declarations, which you can state silently or aloud to affirm Their power and presence within you.

Further Embodying Each Goddess

To support you even more deeply, the Goddesses guided me to share a final section containing more details on them at the end of each gateway. Here is how the information is organized, and how you may make the best use of it:

Origin: What culture/region the Goddess is from.

Also Called: Where applicable, to know Her additional names.

Name Meaning: To connect with Her essence.

Attributes: To better understand Her multifaceted nature as Goddess and the Sacred Feminine aspects of your own nature that She represents.

Sacred Symbols: To appreciate the various symbols that represent the Goddess and to use them in rituals, express them in art, place on your altar, or work with in any way you feel guided.

Chakras: To understand which major energy center(s) the Goddess embodies within you. We have seven major *chakras* (energy wheels) that stack up along the spine as follows:

1. **Root:** Located at the base of the spine/perineum/
   tailbone, and travels down through the legs and
   feet. Its color is red.

2. **Sacral:** Located in the center of the pelvis, womb,
   sexual organs; it is below the navel. Its color is orange.

3. **Solar plexus:** Located in the center of the belly—
   above the navel and below the breastbone. Its color is yellow.

4. **Heart:** Located between the breasts, in the center
   of the chest, it reaches back through the shoulder
   blades. Its traditional color is green, but it can
   also be pink.

5. **Throat:** Located in the hollow center of the collarbone, reaching back to the base of the neck. Its
   color is blue.

6. **Third eye:** Located in the center of the forehead,
   above the eyebrows. Its color is indigo.

7. **Crown:** Located at the top of the head, slightly to
   the back and centered. Its color is violet.

Elements: To understand the natural element or realm
the Goddess inhabits. You may work with the elements
directly if you wish and experience the energetic effects
of these elements as you activate each Goddess.

Essential Oils³: To work with aromatherapy oils specific to each Goddess in your rituals to anoint yourself before an initiation, to use in an oil dispenser, or to use in bath and body care, etc.

Colors: To incorporate the color vibration of each Goddess during initiations through your clothing, candles, altar cloth, or other objects, and to work with after to amplify the Goddess's energy.

Crystals: To work with crystals corresponding to each Goddess by placing them on your altar, in your bath, on your body/*chakras*, or anywhere you feel guided.

Archetype in Balance: To know some of the ways in which the Goddess and Her Sacred Feminine gifts manifest when they are activated in a healthy and harmonious way. To assess which qualities or abilities you already have and which you wish to further cultivate.

Archetype out of Balance: To know some of the ways the Goddess shows up in Her shadow aspect where there is either a deficiency or excess of Her energy. To honestly and compassionately assess if and where you may inhabit or exhibit these imbalances. To see where

---

3   When working with essential oils, it is vital to exercise caution and consult your healthcare practitioner before use if you are pregnant, allergic, or have any other possible contraindications.

you may need to further heal this aspect of the Goddess within yourself or your life.

Creating Balance: To have practices that can help harmonize imbalances and further cultivate the gifts of each Goddess.

Associated Goddesses: To explore additional Goddesses that are connected to and/or complement the Goddess in each gateway.

Prayer/Invocation: To invoke each Goddess as a deity, archetype, or inner aspect of your Sacred Feminine nature to further support the intentions of each initiation.

I hope these additional details, and the entire content and format of each gateway, deeply support you on your path to reclaiming your Goddess nature and unleashing your Sacred Feminine power, beloved.

As you now prepare to begin your journey, know that this book is my heart offering to you and the Goddesses within us all. Every word in it contains my love for you and my reverence for the Goddess you already are. I pray you feel it, sister.

Gateway 1

ENTERING THE VOID

INITIATOR:
SIGE, GODDESS OF SILENCE

Sige

Your hearts know in silence the secrets of the days and the nights.
—Khalil Gibran

The Goddess's first gift to you is nothing. She welcomes you back into the utter emptiness from which it all begins—into Her dark, etheric womb.

To begin to know the Goddess within is to return to the stillness through which all is birthed. It is to release all your dreams and doubts, all your doings and strivings, into Her eternal abyss. It is to completely let go so that you may be completely held in Her all-encompassing embrace as She reveals Her mysteries to you. For it is through emptying yourself of all that is not you that you can come to know who you truly are: a living Goddess.

Such complete surrender also serves as the spiritual foundation to embark and stay on your Divine path so you can learn to let go and let the Goddess heal, guide, and support you in every way.

But it is hard to be still and let go, isn't it, beloved?

We convince ourselves that we don't have time. That we are too busy. That we have too many things to do. Too many people depending on us. Too many tasks demanding

It is through emptying yourself of all that is not you that you can come to know who you truly are: a living Goddess.

from us. We place incessant pressure on ourselves to take care of it all, lest things fall apart. So we keep pushing and doing. But the more we do, the more strife and struggle we create, and the more disconnected we become from our Sacred Feminine gift of pure, empty presence.

In this constant chaos we feel trapped in, we don't stop. We don't rest. We don't pause. We become frazzled, fatigued, and frustrated. If we finally take time off, we may feel guilty about doing nothing. We might feel useless for not being "productive." We may only feel worthy of respite once we've worked ourselves to exhaustion, as if only then do we have the right to rest and retreat. It is as if on some level we don't feel allowed to *just be*.

Or perhaps taking the time to be isn't our actual challenge. As I have experienced on my own journey and found with many of my clients, perhaps it is the deeper fear of *who we will be with* that we try to avoid. For when we enter solitude, we are left with just ourselves. And if we are not well acquainted with ourselves, meeting ourselves can be frightening. Because now we have to face ourselves. And when we do, we may find that getting quiet with ourselves is more threatening than being overwhelmed by life's commotion. We may fear silence if we are afraid of what we might hear in its starkness. We may fear stillness if we are afraid of what we might feel when we finally stop running.

When we sit with ourselves, we have to confront how we really feel about ourselves and our lives. We have to hear what our inner voice is saying and how it speaks to us. When we first become conscious of our thoughts and feelings, we may not like what we uncover. When I teach my clients Goddess meditations, they are usually stunned by the self-negating, critical, and anxious voice they initially confront. As unnerving as this discovery is, the awareness in itself is the first essential step back to our Goddess selves.

Because once we compassionately observe our inner human voice, we create the space necessary for our soul to share its Divine voice. We become receptive to embracing our own Divine nature. We become clear vessels through which our Sacred Feminine gifts can be birthed. And it is in embracing stillness and silence that we can begin to know our Divine nature—our true Goddess selves.

Initiating you on this first sacred step then, beloved, is the Goddess of silence Herself, Sige.

Sige is the Gnostic Mother of All. She is the primordial Goddess of the great void through which all is created. She is the very source of the *aeons*—emanations of the Divine—which she created with Bythos, the God of depth.

Among Her holy children are the male-female pairs of Nous (mind) and

It is in embracing stillness and silence that we can begin to know our Divine nature—our true Goddess selves.

Aletheia (truth), Logos (word) and Zoe (life), and the later female *aeons* Pistis (faith), Elpis (hope), Agape (love), Synesis (intelligence and understanding), Makariotes (bliss), and finally, Sophia (wisdom).

Sige is the stillness through which we feel our spirit.

She is the formless nothingness preceding all form.

She is the dark, fertile cosmic soil through which all sacred thought, truth, word, life, faith, hope, love, understanding, and bliss sprout forth.

Her call to us is subtle, but clear to those who will listen.

Her invitation to us is to hush. Breathe. Retreat. Empty.

THE ART OF BEING

Sige's counsel is to *be* before we *do*. She reminds us that our power isn't achieved through doing—it is released through being. And in this being state of utter emptiness, we are filled with faith, love, and wisdom as it is unleashed from our own sacred centers. She is your Sacred Feminine gifts of intuitive reflection and contemplation that empower your outer action and creation.

Your power isn't achieved through doing—it is released through being.

She is the part of you that knows the wisdom of reflecting before acting so that whatever you do is directed by conscious intention and clear, potent energy rather than approached mindlessly and haphazardly. For everything you do carries the current of the energy you put behind it. Even if you are getting a lot done, if you are disconnected from an inner sense of clarity, peace, and intention, your actions and results will be influenced by this.

However, like Sige, when you surrender to the incubation period that our wombs naturally do when we nurture a baby, you give anything you want to birth—whether it is an inner gift or outer manifestation—the gestation period it needs to form to its fullest potential. Sige is the part of you that welcomes this dark nothingness, because She knows that the void of emptiness is the womb through which all is birthed.

HOLDING SPACE FOR YOURSELF

Sige knows that when we return to Her within our souls through silence and stillness, that on the way to Her we will first meet the tumultuous nature of our minds. And She knows how uncomfortable this initial step can be. But She assures you that if you don't resist but gently witness whatever arises on your way to Her, the voice of your mind will eventually subside and the silence this creates will give way for Her to speak.

Your own Divine voice will begin to share its

mysteries with you, reminding you of all that you truly are and all that you are not. And it will guide you wisely and lovingly on what to do, what not to do, and how to go about it.

When you connect with Sige, you are able to hold space for yourself. And we women need this. This is why we feel lighter and clearer when we share our thoughts and feelings with one another. We need to constantly release our inner turmoil so that we can receive the clear guidance of our hearts and wisdom of our souls. When we share, we don't actually need advice—what we most need from our friends is simply for them to hold space for us as we find the answers within ourselves beneath all the noise. We can so easily offer our empty presence to others, but then neglect to give this to ourselves.

Sige invites you to gift yourself such space, too. When you carve out time and create space for yourself, you offer yourself the essential gift of purging what is overwhelming or over-occupying you in a gentle and loving way.

As you make meeting Her a constant practice through daily meditation or reflection, you invite the loving presence of this wise and mysterious Goddess and allow Her to birth Her infinite gifts through you.

EMBRACING THE MYSTERY

As the Goddess of silence, Sige Herself is shrouded in mystery, and unlike most Goddesses, She reveals very little information about Herself, even in Gnostic texts. This too is an expression of Her (and your) Divine nature and feminine power: in remaining veiled, She silently reveals that She can only be accessed through intuitive experience rather than exoteric understanding.

Sige quietly reminds us that as women, the source of our power does not come from anything outside of us: it comes from the source that rests quietly inside of us, awaiting only our full presence to be unleashed. We are the wombs and vessels for all to be created in our lives, in our world, and in the universe itself. She is here to remind you, beloved, that once you get comfortable in meeting yourself in stillness, you will create the sacred space for all your secret gifts to naturally unfold through you.

She knows that as a woman, you can receive, reflect, release, and replenish when you retreat into sacred silence. All peace awaits you. Every answer is already within you.

It is time to reconnect with Her nature within yourself now, beloved, to receive all Her gifts, and to create a safe space to

We women are the wombs and vessels for all to be created in our lives, in our world, and in the universe itself.

begin your sacred journey. Let go and let Goddess Sige take you now into the silent inner abode so that you may learn the secrets of your soul.

Pre-Initiation Preparation*:

- Come and sit at your altar.

- Light incense or a white or blue candle.

- Although we are entering silence, you are welcome to play soft relaxation music if it helps you delve into meditation.

As with all the initiations, read the script first so that you may follow it during your inner journey.

Sit comfortably in your sanctuary and prepare to enter your inner temple, beloved.

*As my heart-gift, you may download *Sige's Initiation Guided Recording MP3* for FREE at: **FlourishingGoddess.com/sigemp3**

Sige's Initiation: Entering the Void
Ritual type: Guided Meditation

Sitting on the ground or a chair, place your hands on your knees. With palms facing up, bring your fingers into *Buddhi mudra* (gesture of mental clarity) by touching the tips of your pinkies with the tips of your thumbs, keeping your middle three fingers straight.

Close your eyes and rest your awareness on your breath. Notice its gentle, even rhythm as you inhale and exhale.

Focus your *drishti* (inner gaze) on the center of your forehead, where your third eye is located.

Envision a spiral of bluish white light coming from the heavens, descending upon you. Feel this light flow through you, all the way down to your feet.

Now feel or see this spiral of light lifting you up, higher and higher, until you float in the sky.

Feel your mind as calm and clear as this bright blue sky, hovering here for a moment to enjoy its pristine peace.

Sige's spiral lifts you up even higher, beyond this physical time and space, into the inner realms—into the depths of Her boundless heart.

You feel yourself held safely and securely in Her loving embrace.

Let Her hold you, beloved. Give Her all your cares and concerns. Pour your heart out. Tell Her all your hopes and fears, all your worries and concerns. Share everything with Her until there is nothing left.

She receives it all from you without judgment and with unconditional acceptance.

With your permission, She brings forth a column of

light above and through you to free you of all you hold on so tightly to.

Let go. Empty. Purge. Release. Trust. Surrender.

She knows you are weary and She takes it all from you. There is nothing you need to do here. Just be. Just breathe.

Upon this emptying, She fills you with Her love and light. It courses through you, from Her heart into yours, from Her womb into yours. You are filled. You are held. You are blessed.

She shields you in a sphere of light so that you remain safe in your surrender.

Whenever you are ready, Sige releases you back through the ethers, gently and tenderly into the sky once more. Hover here once again, feeling the pull of Mother Earth.

Come all the way back now to your sacred space, filled and surrounded by light.

Feel or imagine roots of light growing from the soles of your feet and base of your spine into the ground, into the core of Mother Earth. You are anchored here now. You are fully back.

Press both palms together in front of your heart, and slowly open your eyes.

You have returned safely from the primordial Mother's womb. And you are welcome to return to Her at any time.

Let Sige be your guide now as She has initiated you into your first step, Goddess.

POST-INITIATION SELF-CARE

- Ground yourself back into your body through light stretching or walking on grass.

- Journal about any thoughts and feelings that came up during your meditation as you will be healing them with the next Goddesses.

- Continue to invoke Sige's column of light when you need to clear your mind, or invoke Her sphere of light to shield your energy.

AFFIRMING SIGE:

In silence, I hear.
In stillness, I feel.
In nothingness, I create.
In emptying, I receive.

I Am Sige.

Goddess Sige

Origin: Gnostic

Name Meaning: Silence

Attributes:

- Silence
- Stillness
- Emptiness
- Wisdom
- Faith
- Truth
- Surrender

- Thought
- Intention
- Oneness
- Clarity
- Peace
- Receptivity

Sacred Symbol: Void

Chakra: Crown

Element: Ether/empty space

Essential Oils:

- Frankincense
- Lavender
- Rosemary
- Sandalwood
- Cedarwood

Color: Black

Crystals:

- Clear quartz
- Selenite

Archetype in Balance:

- Clear, calm mind
- Feels connected to spirit
- Comfortable with silence and own company
- Feels a sense of communion and oneness with all life
- Lives in the present
- Easily receives, trusts, and follows spiritual guidance

Archetype out of Balance:

- Worried
- Anxious
- Restless
- Disconnected with spirituality
- Spacey

- Unfocused
- Overwhelmed
- Easily flustered
- Isolated
- Ungrounded

Creating Balance:

- Create an altar for your spiritual work.
- Meditate daily.
- Take silent retreats.
- Practice mindfulness in everyday moments.
- Bring your awareness to your breath throughout the day.
- Surrender your cares to the Divine.
- Pray.

- Have faith.
- Rest.
- Be still.
- Meditate with the mantras *"Om,"* the universal sound; *"So hum"* to connect with your spirit and all that is; *"Ong namo guru-dev namo,"* to invoke your inner wisdom; or *"Sat nam"* to connect with your true Divine essence.

Associated Goddesses:

- Nemetona (Celtic)
- Aditi (Indian, Hindu)
- Sophia (Gnostic)
- Neith (Egyptian)

Prayer/Invocation:

Beloved Sige, as Goddess of silence within me, I now surrender all cares and concerns to you in exchange for complete clarity and peace. I enter your dark womb so that I may birth my luminescent gifts into being. I silence the noise of my life so that I may hear your voice within.

I am open to perceiving your sacred mysteries as I empty and offer myself as a vessel. Let me now know the secrets of my soul. So be it. So it is.

Gateway 2

Descending into Darkness

Initiators:
Inanna, Goddess of Heaven
&
Ereshkigal, Goddess of the
Underworld

*Inanna &
Ereshkigal*

THERE IS NO BIRTH OF CONSCIOUSNESS WITHOUT PAIN.

—CARL JUNG

The second step on your Goddess path is downward. Deeper, lower, darker, into the shadowy depths of your unconsciousness.

While Sige lifted you up into the ethers and placed you back on earth in a sphere of light, your next two initiatory Goddesses, Inanna and Ereshkigal, will pull you down into the depths of the underworld. They will gently take you through the painful initiatory journey every woman must make—whether of her choosing or not.

This journey is the tempest before the flourishing, where we are stripped of everything we hold dear, left naked, and on our knees. It is the necessary death of our false selves so that we may be born into our true selves—healed and whole.

When it comes without our choosing, this initiation shows up as the abrupt desecration of something foundational: The loss of a job we loathed but relied upon. The end of a toxic relationship. The death of a loved one. The diagnosis of an illness. An accident. An assault.

It is the sudden cracking open of the ground beneath your feet, which forces you to face what lurks beneath. It is a holy invitation to honor your wounds and grieve them fully so that you may invite the grace of healing. It is a benevolently ruthless call to face all the ways in which you have betrayed yourself so that you may find your way back to who you truly are, what you really want, and what you will no longer stand for.

If you are feeling brave, you may embark on this journey when there is no imminent catastrophe in your life but an undeniable inner call to know, heal, and honor all of yourself.

Whether at this moment you are in the midst of such an initiation or descending through your own free will, know this, beloved: *only in facing your darkness can you fully know your light.*

This is why your initiatory Goddesses into this sacred and essential descent are sister Goddesses Inanna and Ereshkigal.

Inanna is an ancient Sumerian Goddess of love, sexuality, fertility, and war. She is Queen of heaven and earth, Goddess of the grain, and the Morning and Evening Star. She is also a prominent figure in some of the oldest recorded myths, including *The Epic of Gilgamesh* (c. 2100–1800 BCE), where She appears as Ishtar.

While benevolent, She is also a Goddess who acts without consideration of consequence, which She pays for with Her very life.

Only in facing your darkness can you fully know your light.

ENTERING THE UNDERWORLD

In Her ancient tale, *The Descent of Inanna* (c. 3500–1900 BCE), Inanna shows up at the gates of the underworld—the domain of her sister, Ereshkigal—demanding to enter so that She may attend Ereshkigal's husband's funeral. As the underworld is forbidden to the living, defying this Divine law is Inanna's first misguided step. The tale opens:

> *From the great heaven the Goddess set Her mind on the great below.*

> *Inanna abandoned heaven and earth to descend to the underworld.*[4]

Interpreting the tale psychologically, Inanna, as Goddess of heaven, represents our conscious and even spiritual selves. Ereshkigal, Goddess of the underworld, represents our unconscious and shadow selves. The warning to us in Inanna's decision to enter the underworld is that when we delve into our unconscious selves, we cannot expect to leave the same person we were when we entered.

Inanna's second misstep was appearing to attend the funeral bedecked in seven pieces of regalia: Her

---

4   J.A. Black, G. Cunningham, J. Ebeling, E. Flückiger-Hawker, E. Robson, J. Taylor, and G. Zólyomi, *The Electronic Text Corpus of Sumerian Literature* (University of Oxford, 1998–2006) http://etcsl.orinst.ox.ac.uk/

shugura (crown), a small lapis lazuli necklace around Her neck, a longer lapis necklace over Her breasts, a royal robe, a breastplate, a gold ring, and a lapis scepter. These regal objects also held Inanna's seven Divine powers. Hearing of Inanna's brazen appearance at Her gates, grief-stricken Ereshkigal reacts by slapping Her own thigh and biting Her lip in rage.

Whether life forces us to make this descent or we embark on it on our own, we may still be holding on to our layers of protection and power and enter feeling entitled rather than surrendered. Since Ereshkigal is in mourning, Inanna's elaborate appearance represents how hurt and betrayed our shadow self feels when we are insensitive to its pain and unwilling to show up tenderly and vulnerably.

Stripping the Layers

In response, Ereshkigal instructs Her chief doorkeeper, Neti, to bolt all the gates and let Inanna in one door at a time, requiring Her to relinquish one of Her cherished belongings at each gate. She demands that Inanna be brought before Her naked and bowed down.

In spite of our best efforts, our shadow self will not tolerate any pretense—material or spiritual. She doesn't care how much money you make or how much you meditate. She requires that you face Her free of all the false notions you hold on to and robbed of the Divine powers you possess.

When Inanna questions why She must relinquish Her precious layers at each gate, She is simply told to be content, be quiet, and not question the ways of the underworld.

When we delve deeper into our inner work, we may resist and question at every level. But our unconscious doesn't follow what is fair and comfortable and demands that we respect its ways if we wish to enter its depths.

DEATH OF THE OLD SELF

By the time She passes through the final gate and faces Her sister, Inanna is naked and bowed low. In spite of this intended humbling, Inanna sees Ereshkigal's vacant throne and begins to make Her way towards it. In Her foolish attempt to take Ereshkigal's throne, Inanna reveals Her true intention for entering the underworld—She plans to rule both Her own and Ereshkigal's realms. This is Inanna's final misstep as it leads to Her immediate judgment and punishment: death.

Often well-meaning wisdom teachings encourage us to overthrow and dethrone our egos and focus only on being "positive" or "spiritual." This may lead us to a misguided desire to gain dominion over our shadow, rather than integrate it into our whole selves.

Now, sentenced to death, Inanna hangs in the underworld as a corpse: *The old self has died.*

But Inanna was wise. Before Her descent, She had instructed her loyal assistant, Ninshubar, to rescue Her with aid from the Gods if She did not return from the underworld in three days' time. Inanna's father, Enki, God of wisdom and water, heeds the plea.

He creates two small creatures, which could pass through the underworld undetected. His first requisite instruction for them is to empathize with Ereshkigal in Her grief. Only once She feels relieved and offers them a gift in gratitude are they to ask for Inanna's corpse so that they can revive her.

Enki represents our higher wisdom, which enables us to redeem ourselves no matter how misguided our steps. Our wise self understands the importance of first acknowledging and empathizing with our grief and pain (our shadow selves), for there to be any chance of reconciliation and resurrection.

The creatures do as instructed. When they find Ereshkigal lamenting, they begin to mirror everything She says with deep compassion and empathy as if Her pain were their own. When She laments, "Oh, my heart!," they cry back, "You are troubled, oh Mistress, oh, your heart!"[5] They continue their wailing with Her until She is finally relieved of Her anguish.

As Enki had predicted, out of gratitude, Ereshkigal offers the creatures a gift, and, as instructed, they ask for Inanna's corpse. Honoring Her word, She gives them Inanna's rotting body. The creatures resurrect Inanna, and Inanna makes Her ascent upward, reclaiming each of Her Divine powers as She progresses through the seven gates.

While Inanna's arrogance kills Her, the sincere empathy offered by two tiny creatures is enough to relieve Ereshkigal from Her pain and grant Inanna new life. And so, it is not our identification with whom and what we think we are that saves us, but the smallest measure of empathy and compassion that sets us free.

At the end of the poem, it is not Inanna, but Ereshkigal who is praised.

This poignant ending reminds us that in the end, credit for Inanna's resurrection doesn't go to Inanna, Her assistant, Her father, or even the creatures of empathy, but to the Queen of the underworld Herself—*to your shadow.*

Your shadow is the Goddess of your underworld. When she feels witnessed and validated, she frees you to rise into your light.

---

5   J.A. Black, G. Cunningham, J. Ebeling, E. Flückiger-Hawker, E. Robson, J. Taylor, and G. Zólyomi, "The Descent of Inanna" in *The Electronic Text Corpus of Sumerian Literature* (University of Oxford, 1998–2006) http://etcsl.orinst.ox.ac.uk/

For your shadow has dominion over your underworld, and when She feels witnessed and validated, She alone has the power to set you free to rise again.

With Inanna—our conscious selves—we may possess the capacity to love, create, and battle, but using our power unconsciously can be fatal to the soul. As She demonstrates, the path back to redemption is to allow ourselves to be stripped of what we didn't honor and reclaim our full selves—shadow and light—with humility, compassion, and reverence.

At this initiation, you will be guided by Inanna Herself, and layer by layer, will have to relinquish parts of yourself at each gate in order to face Ereshkigal—your deepest, darkest pain.

Unlike Inanna, your intention will not be to dethrone your shadow, but, having learned from Inanna's example, you will enter with humility and empathy with the intention to fully witness and embrace this neglected part of yourself.

In your inner journey, each gate will represent the major *chakras*. When we are living in alignment with our full and true selves, each *chakra* is a Divine power we possess. When dishonored, however, we betray ourselves and create deep existential pain.

In your descent, we will strip away all that is not serving you in accordance with your *chakras* and each part of your life so that you may be free to create anew with conscious and unconscious in harmonious union.

For when your shadow self isn't acknowledged, She holds the power to sabotage your best efforts to achieve what you desire. Once you make your peace with Her, however, Her vindication supports and even empowers your intentions and actions.

Let us begin, beloved.

Pre-Initiation Preparation:

- Be sure to have privacy and create sacred space for yourself.

- Keep your journal and pen handy as well as some tissue.

- Begin with a centering meditation with Sige.

- Write the below questions in your journal and answer them honestly.

- Remember, the questions will bring up raw, uncomfortable emotions. Such is the work, beloved. Know that you will be guided by Inanna and Ereshkigal, and held in my prayers at every step. *You can do this.*

Inanna and Ereshkigal's Initiation: Descending into Darkness
Ritual Type: Meditative Journaling

Imagine yourself arriving before sacred gates that mark the entryway into your own underworld. The beautiful Goddess Inanna is here to greet you and welcomes you with tender, sisterly love.

One by one, She cloaks you in seven robes: red, orange, yellow, green, blue, indigo, and violet (the colors of the *chakras*).

She takes your hand and guides you through. You walk down a spiraling staircase and arrive at a door located at the crown of your head. You meet a guard at this first gate, and she asks you:

- How do you neglect your relationship to your spirit and the Divine?

- How do you ignore your truth and the wisdom of your Higher Self?

- How do you create separation between yourself and the universe?

Reflect on these questions, and write the answers in your journal.

Once done, you must surrender your violet robe—all the ways in which you abandon your spirit—to pass through the first gate.

Inanna walks you down the next level of this spiraling stairway, holding your hand tightly and lovingly. You meet the guard at the second gate, in the center of your forehead, and she asks:

- How do you live in fear of the future and stay stuck in the past?

- How do you limit the vision of all that's possible for you?

- How do you dismiss your intuition?

Reflect honestly, and then surrender your indigo robe as you pass through the second gate.

Inanna guides you down, deeper into this dark spiral, and you arrive at the third gate in the soft center of your throat. The guard asks you:

- How do you suppress your authentic feelings and self?

- How do you misuse your words to hurt yourself and others?

- How do you repress your creative expression?

Be radically honest, and then surrender your blue robe to pass through the third gate.

Inanna looks at you with love, and She reminds you that you are not alone here and that it is safe and necessary to keep descending. Arriving at the fourth gate, in the sacred chamber of your heart, the guardian of the gate asks:

- How do you withhold love and compassion from yourself and others?

- How do you prevent yourself from giving and receiving in balance?

- How do you keep your wounds open and bleeding?

Answer her from your heart-truth, even if it hurts, for healing is imminent, beloved. Surrender your green robe as you are allowed through the gate.

Inanna holds you protectively and proceeds to walk before you, delving deeper into the depths of your underworld. Arriving at the fifth gate in the center of your belly, the guard asks:

- How do you give away your power?

- How do you hold yourself back from co-creating what you truly desire?

- How do you play small and dim your light?

You feel these questions pierce through your core and respond from the pit of your stomach. Surrender your yellow robe as you pass through the fifth gate.

Inanna takes you lower, spiraling down into your womb-space. Arriving at this sixth gate, the guard asks:

- How do you deny yourself good: pleasure, passion, joy, abundance, vitality?

- How do you inflict guilt, shame, and self-loathing upon yourself?

- How do you protect yourself from experiencing deep intimacy?

It is so tender here, for you hold so much in your womb. Feel into these questions, beloved, and answer them with brave vulnerability. Surrender your orange robe as the sixth gate opens for you.

Inanna now takes you through the final gate, at the base of your spine, all the way down to the soles of your feet, where the guard asks:

- How do you block yourself from being supported?

- How do you let fear keep you from pursuing your dreams?

- How do you hold yourself back from moving forward?

You answer simply and truthfully, for you have no energy for calculated articulation. With Inanna holding you up, you hand over your red robe and pass through the final gate.

Raw and naked, you finally meet Ereshkigal. She is holding in a sacred embrace your grieving shadow self. See her as a part of you, as a reflection of you. She already knows the pain of all that you have faced at each gate—every part of yourself that you have betrayed—and she is grief-stricken.

She collapses and begins to wail. You immediately fall to your knees, meeting her where she is, and hold her *(you may hold yourself physically here, beloved)*. As she cries out in your arms, you, Inanna, and Ereshkigal cry back with her, repeating with deepest sorrow every wound she is grieving:

All the ways in which she/you have ever been hurt and wronged.

All the wounding that led you to hurt and wrong yourself.

All that you have lost.

All that has been taken from you.

All that you have given up.

Cry with her. Lament with her. Hold her, as you both are held by the Goddesses. Witness her. Accept her. Honor her. Feel her. *Love* her.

Through the light of your unconditional love, she releases all her dark emotions and shares all she so longed to. She purges, until there is nothing left to mourn. You receive it all from her with deepest compassion.

In her own time, she slowly looks up at you, with the glow of relief flowing through her— perhaps for the very first time.

She feels seen, honored, and loved. She finally feels light and free.

You ask her now what she needs from you to continue

to support her. Listen to her needs and promise to honor them, for doing so is the only way to honor *all* of yourself.

Your shadow self thanks you for your humility, courage, and compassion. You both embrace, and there is peace, understanding, and acknowledgment between you.

She stands tall and regal, walks boldly to her throne, and takes her rightful seat. Soothed and collected, she bids you goodbye as you bow to her one more time and turn towards the gates to ascend upward.

Inanna guides the way, so utterly proud of you. Unlike Inanna, however, you do not retrieve your old robes, for they are now the layers of your old self that you have shed. You remain naked as the next step of your journey (along with its initiatory Goddess) requires you to be.

Hold your head up high though, beloved, for you have delved into your deepest, darkest grief, and experienced the alchemy of healing through embracing your shadow self. Your initiation here is complete, and Inanna and Ereshkigal bring you back into your sacred space, fully back into your body, and bless you on your path forward.

POST-INITIATION SELF-CARE:

- Take a few deep, centering breaths to become present in the here and now.

- Bring your palms together in front of your heart, and bow down to yourself, thanking yourself for going on this trying but necessary journey.

- Wake up your body with some gentle stretching, and treat yourself to a nurturing, grounding ritual.

- Re-balance your energy by watching or reading something light and joyful.

AFFIRMING INANNA AND ERESHKIGAL:

I descend.
I die to be reborn.
I bring light into darkness.
I bring darkness into light.

I see my spirit and my shadow.
I feel my joy and my sorrow.
I am all of myself.
I rise.

I Am Inanna. I Am Ereshkigal.

Goddess Inanna

Origin: Sumerian

Name Meaning: Queen of heaven

Attributes:

- Love
- Sex
- Fertility
- Marriage
- Creativity

- Abundance
- War
- Power
- Culture
- Resurrection

Sacred Symbols:

- *Shugura* (crown)
- Regal robes
- Lapis necklace
- Breastplate
- Gold ring
- Lapis scepter
- Shield

- Kohl/eyeliner
- Planet Venus
- Moon
- Roses
- Lion
- Serpent
- Anzu bird

- Trees
- Water (especially rivers and streams)

Chakras:

- Heart
- Solar plexus
- Sacral

Elements:

- Sky/air
- Earth

Essential Oils:

- Rose
- Patchouli
- Geranium
- Ylang-ylang

Colors:

- Lapis blue
- Gold
- Silver
- Red

Crystals:

- Lapis lazuli
- Carnelian
- Ruby
- Citrine
- Tiger's eye

Archetype in Balance:

- Loving
- Empowered
- Stable
- Clear
- Leader

- Passionate
- Service-centered
- Courageous
- Confident

Archetype out of Balance:

- Fickle
- Arrogant
- Impulsive
- Insensitive
- Selfish

- Manipulative
- Stubborn
- Greedy
- Disrespectful

Creating Balance:

- Acknowledge your shadow side.
- Honor your feelings and respect others'.
- Share your gifts and blessings.
- Accept all of yourself.

- Connect and collaborate.
- Be grateful for what you already have.
- Serve others with your gifts.

- Consult your inner wisdom.

- Be willing to see and respect other's views and values while honoring your own.

- Be confident but humble.

Associated Goddesses:

- Ishtar (Mesopotamian)

- Astarte (Canaanite)

- Aphrodite (Greek)

- Isis (Egyptian)

- Venus (Roman)

- Hera (Greek)

Prayer/Invocation:

Beloved Inanna, as Queen of heaven within me, grant me the courage to face all that I need to with reverence and humility. Let me open to the healing that can only happen by honoring and accepting all of myself unconditionally. Let me find the wisdom within my wounds so that I may arise whole and renewed. So be it. So it is.

Goddess Ereshkigal

Origin: Sumerian

Name Meaning: Queen of the underworld

Attributes:

- Shadow-work
- Grief
- Healing
- Death
- Judgment
- Envy

- Wrath
- Compassion
- Discernment
- Mercy
- Power
- Transformation

Sacred Symbols:

- Gates
- Stairs
- Tears

- Underworld
- Lion
- Serpent

Chakras:

- Throat
- Heart

- Solar plexus

Element: Underworld

Essential Oils:

- Roman chamomile
- Grapefruit
- Mimosa

Colors: Black

Crystals:

- Apache tear
- Onyx
- Carnelian
- Sugilite
- Rose quartz
- Ruby in moonstone
- Red tiger's eye

Archetype in Balance:

- Self-aware
- Secure
- Empowered
- Discerning
- Easily sets boundaries
- Compassionate
- Honest
- Wise

Archetype out of Balance:

- Victim
- Drama queen
- Self-loathing
- Depressed
- Cold/merciless

- Easily triggered
- Untrusting
- Competitive
- Envious
- Territorial

Creating Balance:

- Journal about your feelings.
- Work with a heart-centered therapist, coach, or healer to process your grief.
- Love and honor all of yourself.
- Do inner child, past life, shadow, and grief healing work.
- See and honor your light.

- Practice self-compassion.
- Set healthy boundaries.
- Transform envy into inspiration.
- Replace competition with collaboration.
- Know your divine worth.
- Take back your power.

Associated Goddesses:

- Persephone (Greek)
- Sedna (Native American)
- Lilith (Mesopotamian)
- Nephthys (Egyptian)
- Hecate (Greek)
- Baba Yaga (Russian)
- Hella (Norse)

Prayer/Invocation:

Beloved Ereshkigal, as Queen of the underworld within me, help me to feel my pain and grief fully. No matter how old or deep, let my wounds be revealed so that I may be fully restored and healed. Let me see and embrace my shadow self so that I may love and honor all of myself. Let me transcend all victimhood so that I may arise victorious. So be it. So it is.

Gateway 3

Unleashing Your Wrath

Initiator:
Pele, Goddess of Transformation

Pele

BITTERNESS IS LIKE CANCER.
IT EATS UPON THE HOST.
BUT ANGER IS LIKE FIRE.
IT BURNS IT ALL CLEAN.
—MAYA ANGELOU

Here you are, beloved. Naked, raw, and exposed. Guided, loved, and blessed.

As you have ascended like Inanna from the depths of the underworld, feeling and honoring your grief, you are now ready to be initiated through your next sacred gateway: *owning your righteous wrath.*

As women, we are not encouraged to get angry. We are taught since we are little girls to be polite and play nice. As we get older and seek helpful ways to manage our anger, we find that even spiritual teachings advise us to simply observe it and let it go. Here is a quote that came my way today, shared by His Holiness the Dalai Lama (someone I deeply respect) with his social media followers:

Anger may seem to be a source of energy, but it's blind. It causes us to lose our restraint. It may stir courage, but again it's blind courage. Negative emotions, which often arise from a spontaneous impulse, cannot be justified by reason, whereas positive emotions can.

But as your next initiatory Goddess is here to show

you, denying this most natural and primal emotion is akin to attempting to extinguish a volcano: it will either die inside, killing a primal and vital part of your feminine nature, or, when least expected, it will erupt full force and destroy everything around it. And while this destruction may seem chaotic and ruthless, it is also transformative and regenerative, beloved.

Pele, the Hawaiian Goddess of fire and volcanoes and Creatress of the islands, is here to remind you that *your anger is sacred*. Her name, *Ka-ula-o-Keah*, means "the redness of the fire." In one of Her origin myths, Pele is killed by Her ocean Goddess sister and finds refuge in the pit of the volcano of Mount Kilauea. Through its lava fires, Pele's soul was revived and She continues to live there to receive and regenerate the souls of the dead.

Pele is both a Destructress and Creatress. She birthed Her heavenly Hawaiian islands through the molten lava of Her hellish fires—linked to both Her passion and ire.

Her unpredictable and uncontrollable power is the primal life force and is both feared and venerated among Her people. Whether Her eruptions arise from Her delight or rage, when Pele blows Her breath of fire, She incinerates everything along Her path and then dances Her dance of creation to birth life anew.

She will not tolerate exploitation and disrespect. According to a recently popularized twentieth century myth, it is said that those who take lava rock, pumice, or sand from Hawaii to their homelands will incur "Pele's curse" and experience a stream of bad luck until they return the materials to Her native land. She protects what is sacred to Her, destroys what doesn't serve Her, and creates what pleases Her.

She is *shakti*—the primordial feminine life-force—embodied. Perhaps it is this untamable and transformative nature of feminine power that our anger is so vehemently stifled, even by enlightened spiritual teachers.

But, like Pele, you have a volcano inside of you that must be honored, lest you lose your primal connection to your own feminine force. Pele is here to teach you that your wrath is the molten lava that erupts from the pit of your volcanic belly to transform and transmute what is not in alignment with your truth:

- The boss who bullies you.

- The colleague who sabotages you.

- The friend who uses you.

- The parent who dismisses you.

- The partner who neglects you.

- The you who denies you.

Your wrath is the lava that erupts from the pit of your volcanic belly to transform and transmute all that is not in alignment with your truth.

It is the breaking point beyond all patience that finally elicits the rightful response: *Enough*. Thankfully, I have had many such eruptions in my own life:

- Saying enough to my parents' abuse towards my siblings and me.

- Saying no to an arranged marriage at the age of seventeen.

- Saying no to demands to wear a *hijab* (Islamic head covering).

- Saying no to being forbidden to pursue post-secondary education.

- Saying enough to a relationship with an uncommitted partner.

- Saying enough to bosses who constantly bullied and a soul-sucking corporate career.

None of these moments were comfortable, and all of them were terrifying. And when my voice shook, when my heart raced, when my knees buckled, it was my righteous rage that ignited from the core of my being that gave me the strength I needed to overcome my oppressors.

Such is the power that lies at the core of every woman. There is an uncontrollable force that clears your path and cleanses your life so that you may create a new world for yourself, blazing with your primal passion.

One of the many reasons such feminine power is often oppressed is because of its ferocious, rampant nature. A volcano cannot be wielded to one's will. Even the most dormant volcano must be revered and respected, for you never know when she will have her own "Enough!"

Even the most comprising woman—one who might feel so disconnected from her sacred self-worth that she stays in toxic and even abusive relationships—can, with Pele's grace, be pushed to her limit and unleash her wrath on the instigator without warning or mercy. And thus, the fire of her rightful rage can finally set her free.

It is your Divine right to protect what is sacred to you, beloved. And sometimes, doing so requires summoning your righteous rage. This does not entitle you to violate or abuse others. Rather, it is about finally giving yourself permission to first feel your wrath, and then consciously harness it to make courageous choices and empowered changes. It is a potent path to connect with your unbridled power and channel it to transform what no longer serves you.

Like honoring our grief with Inanna and Ereshkigal, owning our anger is also essential to our healing. Unprocessed anger can turn into resentment,

Your righteous wrath clears your path and cleanses your life.

which becomes toxic and even poisonous to our minds, bodies, and souls.

Often, we feel uncomfortable facing our anger because it doesn't feel like an evolved or spiritual reaction. Sometimes, when it involves our parents or loved ones, we can even carry too much guilt to feel anger towards them. But suppressing our anger keeps us stuck and stagnant, while embracing it frees us in a way that the more "positive" emotions can fall short of.

In fact, on my own healing journey and the transformations I am blessed to facilitate for my clients, I don't even consider working on forgiveness (which is also imperative to our healing) until we first fully uncover and express our repressed rage.

So, my love, as Pele guides you into your own inner volcano, be unafraid of the lava that has been yearning to explode. For fire is the element that transforms lead into gold, and your ire is that fire.

PRE-INITIATION PREPARATION:

- Ensure you have complete privacy for this ritual.

- Choose a space in your home where you can freely move and dance.

- If you want, you can practice this ritual naked.

- Find some intense, primal music and/or Polynesian chants that will help you get in touch with your rage, and keep this ready for your ritual. Have a soft relaxation track handy as well.

- Light some orange and red candles, and place them somewhere safe where you can see them, but where they won't be disturbed.

- Play your music and prepare to unleash your wrath.

Pele's Initiation: Unleashing Your Wrath
Ritual Type: Movement Meditation

Lying down, take some deep belly breaths as you summon your inner fire. Begin to call into your conscious awareness events and experiences where you were betrayed, used, disrespected, abandoned, and wronged.

You have already felt the grief of these experiences with Inanna and Ereshkigal. If you need to go back there, feel free to return to their initiation ritual.

If you feel ready to get angry, Pele is here to receive you. She lifts you from where you are lying and into the core of Her volcano.

Rising slowly, let your body move in unison with the sound of your music. Inhale and exhale deeply, sharply, and loudly from the pit of your belly. Feel the fires of lava dance around you in rapture as you summon your deepest rage.

Begin to dance around the room with Pele, knowing you are simultaneously dancing with Her in Her sacred volcano, connected in both the physical and spiritual realms in this holy instant.

Feel the lava bubbling and rising from inside you, ready to erupt through your core. Feel the rage, which is your sacred right to feel, towards every person and situation that ever dishonored you. *Shake, howl, and dance it out!*

Pele joins you in your dance of wrath as your volcanic ire erupts fully from every cell of your being. You have full permission to explode. Scream. Swear. Sigh.

Dance your dance of wrath until every spark of rage finds its righteous release.

Behold the sight of your erupted volcano. Behold all this pent up energy finally purged and free! Its fire transforms all the experiences that gave rise to your rage. It clears all the patterns in your own consciousness that called these experiences in for your growth and evolution. It transmutes all false and negative conclusions you made about your own worth and value because of what happened to you—because of what *they* did or didn't do to you.

When you feel all has been released through your sacred dance and volcanic eruption, let the fires settle. Slow the pace of your dance. Lower the volume of the music or change to a softer track. Lie down again with your hands gently resting on your belly.

Pele sits with you and places Her hands on your belly too, keeping the light of your inner fire burning bright. This is your power center, your solar plexus *chakra*. And while it held the power to erupt into a volcano, Pele reminds you that it is not enough to just release your rage. It is essential to replace the old patterns that gave rise to it with ones that will honor you instead.

With Her hands sealing your healing in a sphere

of golden light around your center, Pele implores you now, with fierce maternal love:

"What do you deserve?

"What will you no longer tolerate?

"What will you expect and command instead?"

As you contemplate this, tuning into the wisdom of your body, heart, and soul to receive your truth and answers, Pele seals your solar plexus with a sphere of golden light until it shines like a flaming sun.

She rises and moves gracefully around you, gently calming the lava fires, for She is also Goddess of wind. She breathes Her maternal *shakti* breath all over this sacred fire until it cools and turns into dark, rich lava rock.

With Pele's blessing, you have now created a new foundation for yourself. Through the powerful release of your own inner fire, you have cleared the old and paved the path to create anew in alignment with what will serve and honor you.

Slowly sitting up, look around your sacred island in Pele's realm. Know that you are preparing for a fresh start, one in which no one will dare to dishonor you— including yourself.

In gratitude and reverence, bring your hands together in front of your heart, and bow down to yourself and Pele for honoring your Divine right to own and unleash your Divine wrath. This is your Sacred Feminine power, and it is yours to own and wield at *your* will.

POST-INITIATION SELF-CARE

- You may wish to write down any of the memories or emotions that came up in your dance, and then safely burn the paper in sacred release.

- If you practice sage smudging, it would be wonderful to clear yourself and your space with a smudging ritual now.

- When you have completed your fiery rituals, extinguish any lit candles and sage.

- You may also wish to write your inner reflections and answers on what you desire and deserve instead, as you will create new honoring relationships and empowering patterns for yourself. Record these in your journal, as you will gain the courage to honor them with our next Goddess.

- When your initiation is complete, practice a nourishing grounding ritual.

- Wear red or orange to continue to honor Pele within.

Affirming Pele:

Behold the power of my righteous ire
Beware the breath of my inner fire.
Tread carefully upon my sacred lands
Lest you unleash what you cannot withstand.

I Am Pele.

Goddess Pele

Origin: Hawaiian

Name Meaning: The redness of fire

Attributes:

- Sacred rage
- Destruction
- Creation
- Transformation
- Regeneration
- Dance
- Primal power
- Instinct
- Passion
- Raw emotions

Sacred Symbols:

- Volcano
- Islands
- Rain
- Lightning
- Dance
- Smoke

Chakras:

- Solar plexus
- Sacral

Elements:

- Fire
- Air/wind
- Thunder/lightning

Essential Oils:

- Clove
- Cinnamon
- Ginger
- Sweet orange

Colors:

- Yellow
- Orange
- Red
- Black

Crystals:

- Amber
- Lava rock
- Citrine

Archetype in Balance:

- Passionate
- Powerful
- Creative
- Expressive
- Flourishing
- Honest
- Empowered

Archetype out of Balance:

- Angry
- Stifled
- Resentful
- Passive aggressive
- Mean
- Vengeful
- Jealous

Creating Balance:

- Clear your energy with a primal dance.
- Process your anger safely through journaling, ritual, or therapy/coaching.
- Speak your truth clearly.
- Do what you love.
- Uncover and enjoy your passions.
- Make time for creative projects.
- Practice the breath of fire.
- Get clear on your values and desires.
- Honor your priorities.
- Protect what is sacred to you.
- Use fire in rituals through smudging, incense, and burning letters of what you want to release.

Associated Goddesses:

- Sekhmet (Egyptian)
- Gaia (Greek)
- Brigid (Celtic)
- Freya (Norse)

Prayer/Invocation:

Beloved Pele, as the Goddess of transformation within me, let the fires of my sacred rage burn and transmute all that no longer serves me. Let me unleash my Divine feminine power to destroy the old and create anew. Let me dance my desires into creation with fiery delight! So be it. So it is.

Gateway 4

CONQUERING YOUR FEARS

INITIATOR:
KALI, GODDESS OF POWER

Kali

AMONG THE GODDESSES WHO
COMPRISE THE GREAT FEMININE,
KALI IS THE LAST LINE OF DEFENSE
FOR THE WORST EVILS. WHERE
LESSER POWER FAILS,
KALI OVERCOMES.
—NAMADEVA ACHARYA

You have done so well, my beloved sister. You have been so bravely vulnerable through your initiations with the benevolent dark Goddesses, who relish in the stripping and burning of all that is not truly you.

And yet, there may still be a part of you that feels unworthy of being the Goddess that you already are. There may still be a part of you that fears shaking things up. There may still be a part of you that is clinging to what feels familiar and comfortable—even as you know your soul is ready to soar.

This is why the next gateway into your Sacred Feminine power is to summon your inner Warrioress to overcome your most unrelenting fears. Initiating you into this sacred step could be none other than the ultimate Warrior Goddess Herself: Kali.

On the surface, Kali is a ferocious Hindu Goddess who delights in death and destruction. Her images as a dark, multi-limbed Warrioress typically depict Her armed with Her ruthless sword, proudly adorned with a garland of skulls, and holding a severed head. Her snakey black hair flails wildly, Her tongue hangs out in bloodlust. At first glance, it is only fair to shudder at Her sight.

But, like us women, Kali is a lot more complex and multidimensional when we dare to delve deeper into Her mysteries. Her name derives from the Sanskrit root "kala," meaning time. Yet Kali is beyond time: She is the devourer of time. She is the abyss into which all illusion is dissolved and turned into the nothingness it truly is. She is the Dark Mother who aborts your false self in Her timeless womb only to rebirth you into who you truly are: Goddess manifest.

In one of Her origin stories, She sprung from warrior Goddess Durga's forehead at the last minute when defeat appeared imminent. Durga Herself emerged from the collective powers of great celestial beings to battle an indestructible demon and his army of minions. Her legion of Warrioresses (called *Matrikas*) were able to defeat the horde while Durga focused Her full attention on the demon. As Durga slayed the demon—like the myth of the Greek hydra—each drop of blood led to the demon reproducing its heads.

As the demon kept multiplying, in a moment of utter despair, Durga summoned all Her might and shot out war-hungry

> *Kali is the Dark Mother who aborts your false self in Her timeless womb only to rebirth you into who you truly are: Goddess manifest.*

and blood-thirsty Kali from the center of Her forehead. Kali started ferociously slaying the demon's heads and instantly drank every drop of blood it dripped. As She slayed all his heads, Kali started stringing them around Her neck in ecstatic celebration.

She fervently continued Her carnage until the ultimate demon was obliterated. It is his head that She proudly holds in Her hand as She dances Her dance of victory.

Looking more closely at Her story, Kali's terrifying nature becomes a source of resolve and resilience for us women. Her springing from Durga's forehead (the third eye and abode of spiritual wisdom) reminds us that in our darkest moments of despair—when it seems our fears will surely overcome us—we can invoke our single-pointed focus and fearless Warrioress to slay our most unyielding demons.

While Pele's element of transformation is Her sacred fire, Kali's is Her sword of truth. Wielding Her sword as She wills, She cuts through our attachments and illusions with merciful ruthlessness for our own liberation and expansion. As the loving and fiercely protective Mother, She will sever our self-sabotaging patterns in the most abrupt, uncomfortable, and effective means necessary. Her bloodlust is the passionate thirst required to revel in destroying our demons.

Kali will make you face your deepest fears and ego identifications so that you can finally come to know who you truly are and how loved, guided, and protected you always are.

And this is the essential step on your path now, beloved. Because before you can meet the light Goddesses to rise up and flourish, you must allow the dark Goddesses to clear the way.

As we have entered into the Goddess's silent womb to surrender your thoughts, navigated the depths of the underworld to face your grief, and erupted through a volcano to transform your wrath, summoning the fierce grace of Kali is now called upon to free you of your fears.

Kali bursts into our lives to keep us on our Divine right paths when She sees that we did not heed life's gentler nudges. If there is one thing I have learned from this most merciful Mother, it is that if we don't face our fears and honor our truth on our own, She will have no qualms in forcing us to.

If you fear failure, She will get you fired from your toxic day job so that you can finally commit to your calling.

If you fear success, She will make someone else thrive with *your idea* so that you finally believe in yourself enough to follow your inspirations.

If you fear being abandoned, She will make you catch your partner in an act of betrayal so that you can learn to be loyal to yourself.

If you fear rejection, She will have others chosen over you so you can heal your lack of self-worth.

If you fear scarcity, She will make you lose your material security so that you can remember that the Divine within is the true and only source of your sustenance, and this loving source will *always* provide.

If you fear uncertainty, She will tear down the pillars of your secure life until you learn to create your outer world from an inner foundation of unbreakable faith.

If you fear authority, She will bring tyrants upon your path until you finally summon the courage to stand your ground and claim your power.

Whatever your fears, Kali will not stand by as you let them rule your realm.

It is time to face them now, beloved. It is time to summon your own ferocious Warrioress to slay your demons so that you may be free to dance with abandon in the swirling abyss of life.

PRE-INITIATION PREPARATION:

- Find some Kali mantra chants to play during your ritual.

- If you want, like Kali, you can be naked and let your hair run loose (ensure you have space and privacy for this).

- Light black or dark blue candles in a safe space.

- Burn incense in Her honor.

KALI'S INITIATION: CONQUERING YOUR FEARS
Ritual Type: Guided Meditation

Prepare your sacred space with the incense and Kali's mantra music, and then center yourself with a quick Sige meditation.

Keeping your eyes closed in meditation, imagine your bubble of light transporting you into the inner realms. Finding yourself in the dark temple of Kali, invoke Her with Her mantra, *"Om Klim Kalika-Yei Namaha"* three times.

Feel Her instant presence with you, permeating through your being as fierce love and power. Kali stands ready, sword in hand and tongue hanging out, to dance with you.

She gives you your own sword of light, and playfully invites you to join Her on Her temple grounds.

Feeling completely safe in Her presence, you begin to dance with Her, playing with your swords and sticking out your tongues.

As you dance, Kali asks you to be unafraid to face your deepest, darkest fears.

Knowing Her protection is impenetrable, you share your first, most pestilent fear with Her. As soon as you do, it appears before you both, taking on form. You see a chord connecting you to your fear, through which it depletes you of your Divine power.

You demand your fear to speak and listen to it express its true essence:

I am your Insecurity!
I am your Self-loathing!
I am your Unworthiness!
I am your Jealousy!
I am your Greed!
I am your Doubt!
I am your Scarcity!
I am your Attachment!
I am your Anxiety!

As you face your fear in its purest form, Kali places

Her hands on your heart and head, connecting you to your Divine wisdom. In response to every fear and one with your eternal inherent truth, you declare back, "My truth is ____."

Or, if it works better for you, you can affirm, "My heart says ____." Or, "My soul knows ____." Let the clear, precise, unfiltered truth emerge through you, as Kali did from Durga's third eye.

If you are unsure of whether or not you are hearing your truth, stay with the process, beloved. Keep saying one of the truth provocations, and trust that the truth will flow through.

When you express your truth statement with your sword of light, Kali fills you with Her Warrioress resolve, and you swiftly swing it in front of you, severing the toxic cord that binds you to your fear. As you do, Kali and you dance your dance of destruction and obliterate your fear until it dissolves into nothingness and remains forever in Kali's eternal abyss.

One by one, you keep calling forth each and every one of your fears. As you notice the cord that attached you both, feel into how this fear drains you, sabotages you, and overpowers you.

Then feel fully into the infinite strength of your spirit and essence of your Divine nature as you declare your truth in response to your fear. As soon as you affirm your truth, you cut the cord and dance with Kali until all the remnants of your fear are cleared and transmuted.

With each victory, you feel more and more empowered, wild, and free. You begin to relish in this sacred battle, slaying your inner demons with bloodlust and rapture.

You feel yourself growing more arms so you can swiftly obliterate all your fears until they are all faced and conquered. You see yourself growing larger and larger until, like Kali, you take up the cosmos and your fears are but pests at your feet. You trample them into oblivion and delight in unleashing your fierce feminine force.

When you feel all your fears are overcome, begin to slow your Warrioress dance. As you come to stillness, Kali reminds you that your courage comes not from the absence of these fears, but from your willingness to constantly face and defeat them with the Divine truths your heart and soul arm you with.

You thank Kali for Her infinite maternal love and endless protection and slowly return back to your physical size. Kali remains vast and boundless. She smiles and begins to glow, revealing Her true luminescent nature to you as the Divine Mother. You feel overcome by Her love and compassion and melt into Her arms, which enfold you in bliss.

In Her arms, you come back into the present and embrace yourself as She does—with unconditional love.

Bringing your palms together in front of your heart,

thank yourself and Kali *Ma* (Mother Kali) as you come fully back, and open your eyes.

You have now done the scariest thing: you have faced and boldly conquered your deepest, darkest fears. You have finally freed yourself from their hold over you. You have reclaimed your Divine nature and power. You have awakened the ultimate Warrioress within, beloved.

Now, after some essential post-initiation self-care, you will be ready for your next initiation with a Goddess who is equally as loving, but much gentler in Her approach.

POST-INITIATION SELF-CARE:

- Anchor yourself with a grounding ritual.

- Write down your fears and your heart truths so that you can face your fears and own your truth.

- You may tear up the page with your fears (honoring Kali's element of air) and then safely burn them for further transmutation.

- Affirm your truth declarations to yourself, and even read them to yourself before bed to let their essence permeate through your consciousness.

- Honor your truth by ensuring your actions align with the truth of who you are.

AFFIRMING KALI:

Your fears may be dark
But I am darker still
I whose womb becomes the tomb
Of every demon we kill.

I Am Kali.

Goddess Kali

Origin: Indian

Name Meaning: Black one, Time, The fullness of time, Timelessness

Attributes:

- Transformation
- Liberation
- Radical change
- Destruction
- Fearlessness
- Overcoming ego
- Detachment

- Surrender
- Freedom .
- Perseverance
- Warrioress
- Wildness
- Empowerment
- Endings and beginnings

Sacred Symbols:

- Sword
- Blood

- Skulls
- Lotus

Chakras:

- Crown
- Third Eye
- Solar plexus

Element: Air

Essential Oils:

- Juniper
- Fennel
- Vetiver

Colors:

- Black
- Red
- Dark blue

Crystals:

- Black onyx
- Bloodstone
- Hematite
- Black obsidian
- Red jasper
- Black tourmaline
- Red tiger's eye

Archetype in Balance:

- Surrenders to transformation
- Does not tolerate toxic situations
- Independent
- Focused
- Determined
- Courageous
- Knows oneself as a spiritual being

- Unattached to material outcomes/situations
- Strong
- Resilient
- Welcomes change
- Revolutionary
- Leader

Archetype out of Balance:

- Angry
- Volatile
- Aggressive
- Cruel
- Unstable
- Attached to outcome

- Complacent
- Resistant to change
- Identified with ego
- Stuck
- Fearful

Creating Balance:

- Let go of what no longer serves you.
- Embrace change.

- Release attachment to outcome.

- Appreciate the material without attachment.

- Reclaim your Divine nature as an eternal Divine being.

- Summon your inner Warrioress.

- Trust in Divine will and timing.

- Speak your truth.

- Cut energetic cords with toxic relationships.

- Clear your energy through yoga.

- Honor your Divine path.

- Invoke Kali through Her mantras, *"Om Kleem Kalika-yei Namaha."*

- Shield your energy with protective light.

- Lead the way for change and revolution.

Associated Goddesses:

- Durga (Indian)

- Green Tara (Buddhist)

- Sekhmet (Egyptian)

Prayer/Invocation:

Beloved Kali Ma, *as the Goddess of power within me, help me to face and overcome my deepest, darkest fears so that I may be free and powerful like you. I am willing to release all that no longer serves me. Wield your sword of light to cut through all my ego illusions and sever all toxic, disempowering attachments.*

I am ready to move forward courageously, connected to, centered in, and living from my Divine, eternal truth. Protect, guide, and bless me through this sacred transformation. I am ready. I am yours. Om Kleem Kalika-yei Namaha. Om Shanti, Shanti, Shanti. *So be it. So it is.*

Gateway 5

RISING AS THE LOTUS

INITIATOR:
KUAN YIN, GODDESS OF COMPASSION

Kuan Yin

> FORGIVENESS IS A SILENT,
> INTIMATE TEACHER. SHE IS ALWAYS
> READY TO BRING THE LESSONS
> YOU NEED, WHETHER OR NOT YOU
> WANT TO LEARN.
>   —IYANLA VANZANT

My deepest bows of love to you, beloved sister, for being here now. You have felt fully and fought courageously. And now, it is time to rest. It is time to float on the lotus waters of compassion with your next initiatory Goddess: Kuan Yin.

As the Goddess of mercy, grace, and wisdom, Kuan Yin is here to hold you ever so tenderly to wash away any remaining pain, resentment, or darkness in your heart and being so that you may be free to move forward and flourish.

The gateway to awakening your Sacred Feminine gift of compassion is through the grace of forgiveness. After meeting yourself in silence, feeling your grief, releasing your rage, and conquering your fears, your journey back to wholeness would be incomplete without this essential step.

Forgiveness is an interesting area for us women. On the one hand, we may feel compelled to forgive a transgression instantaneously without first processing our rightful grief and anger. But as this darkness goes unacknowledged, it can turn into physical and emotional *dis-ease* within us over time.

On the other hand, we might hold on to our sorrow and rage and justify withholding forgiveness because "they don't deserve it." Where in the first instance it is the negating of our darker emotions that can lead to disease, in this case, it is our obsessive attachment to it that can harm us.

In both cases, it is essential to own and process our grief and rage as a preliminary step to free ourselves through forgiveness. When grief and rage aren't felt and released, they turn into victimhood and bitterness. But when we process them in a safe and thorough way as we have with the previous Goddesses, it frees up our energy to be re-channeled in more empowering and self-honoring ways. And the final part of this healing journey requires forgiveness.

That said, I fully understand that sometimes others' actions, indeed, feel unforgivable. When I looked back at the men who sexually assaulted me during my childhood, I couldn't fathom forgiveness when I thought of doing it *for them*.

But then I realized that by carrying the pain, shame, and self-loathing that *their* actions constantly triggered within me, that it was me—not them—who continued to suffer long after their acts. I knew I

Forgiveness is not something we do for the other, but a gift we give to ourselves.

needed and deserved to forgive *for myself.* And so, my love, forgiveness is not something we do for the other, but for ourselves.

What shifts everything is remembering that forgiveness is a decision to get unstuck and free up all that energy and power that you gave away to those who hurt or wronged you, and reclaim it for yourself.

It is a reclamation that *I deserve to be free. I deserve to have a whole, happy heart, and a full, flourishing life.*

And if you need sacred support on this part of your path, you are so beneficently guided by the Goddess of forgiveness Herself, the benevolent Kuan Yin.

Her unconditional love for all beings and Her ability to come to everyone's aid is perhaps why She is often referred to as "the most widely Beloved Buddhist divinity."[6]

Kuan Yin is the feminine manifestation or counterpart to Avalokiteshwara, a male *bodhisattva* (a being ready for enlightenment but delaying it) of infinite compassion. In either female or male form, they are Divine beings who hear the suffering of the world and have vowed not to ascend to full Buddhahood until they help all sentient beings attain enlightenment.

As a Goddess of the people, She is venerated all over East and Southeast Asia and is very popular in Chinese folk communities. One of the folk myths I find especially

6   *Encyclopedia Britannica Online*, s.v. "Avalokiteshvara." https://global.britannica.com/topic/Avalokiteshvara

inspiring for us women tells of Kuan Yin as the young daughter of a governor who kept Her confined to their home. One day, She managed to escape the premises and found Her way to a monastery that She previously could only admire from Her room.

As She began to explore what She considered to be a sanctuary, She suddenly found Herself surrounded by a gang of corrupt monks. Slowly, they forced Her into a hidden chamber and mercilessly took turns raping Her.

When Her father got word that a girl was seen entering the temple that day, he assumed that Kuan Yin had escaped to meet a secret lover. In blind rage and pride, he ordered the monastery to be burnt to the grounds, and anyone attempting to escape was to be killed on sight.

As the governor tried to alleviate his guilt the next day, Kuan Yin appeared to him in a glowing haze and spoke to Her father. She told him what had happened to Her at the monastery and that despite the unconscious acts of all the men responsible for Her tragic end, She had pity on them and forgave them completely.

She proceeded to tell him that while the temple burned, She was lifted to the realm of the celestials. There, She was elevated to the status of Goddess, upon which She vowed to help all beings who suffered as She had. Her name was changed to *Kuan Shi Yin Pusa*, which means "She who hears the cries of the world."

It is no wonder that Kuan Yin is often shown

floating on a beautiful lotus flower, as, like the lotus, She exemplifies rising above the murky waters of life's trials—pure of heart and untainted in spirit.

Given my own experience with men who violated me as a child and with a father who brutally beat me the first time he learned I had been assaulted, forgiving these men as Kuan Yin did so instantly and gracefully seemed an impossible task.

When we look closer at Kuan Yin's nature, however, what She truly teaches us is that She forgives not because the acts of Her perpetrators were redeemable, but because She knows that those who inflict suffering are also suffering. This is not in any way to justify or condone horrible acts. Instead, it is to know that forgiveness is an understanding that people act at the level of consciousness on which they are operating, and that to expect something else from them only makes *us suffer*.

Forgiving means that we set those who have hurt or wronged us free on their own soul journeys so that we may be free on ours. It means we take back our Divine peace, power, and purity and radiate it out in blessing to all, without exception.

Beyond releasing our pain, Kuan Yin shows us that the deeper grace comes as we choose to create growth, extract lessons, and find wisdom from our traumas while surrendering everything else to the Divine for healing and purification.

When we refuse to find the lesson that life may be

teaching us through our painful experiences, we may unconsciously, energetically, and even karmically continue to call in similar experiences until we learn the lesson our soul intends for us to learn.

This does not mean that we are to blame ourselves for creating our struggles. Rather, it is about switching from an unconscious victim-mode reaction of, "Why did this happen to me?" or "Why does this keep happening to me?" to a more empowered, conscious response of: "What does my soul want me to learn from this?" or "What lesson is this person/experience here to teach me?"

Where the first reaction makes you feel powerless, the second response empowers you to find the grace in the experience and move forward with strength and wisdom.

We can also view our perpetrators as spiritual teachers. Though as women, we need to be careful with this. Many of my deeply loving, sensitive, and compassionate clients share with me that they feel they need to stay in toxic, unbalanced, or even abusive relationships with people because they feel they need to learn how to unconditionally love, accept, and forgive them. They even profess to believing that leaving or "abandoning" these people would be selfish and "unspiritual."

But Kuan Yin as the Goddess of compassion and spiritual wisdom within you does not condone staying in dishonoring situations. She reminds you that loving and accepting others unconditionally does not mean unconditionally accepting their unloving acts.

While She invites you to see anyone who has or is hurting you as also hurting themselves, She also implores you to have unconditional love and compassion for yourself. In doing so, She invites you to forgive the person, learn the lesson your soul would have you learn as a result of your experience with them, and then either evolve your relationship or evolve yourself beyond it.

Sometimes, by you bringing awareness to how their actions are hurting you, they may seek your forgiveness and be willing to act more consciously and lovingly as you both move forward. And sometimes, if they refuse to or are unable to (such as if they have passed away or otherwise can't) treat you as you deserve to be, then you can gracefully float forward on your lotus flower, blessing and releasing them on their paths. You can thank them for being a spiritual teacher on your own soul's journey and free yourself of the need to have similar people or experiences show up as you rise above your past with them.

Like Kuan Yin, when we approach the stories of what happened to us with an intention to see how our painful experiences actually happened *for us*, we begin to see opportunities

Loving and accepting others unconditionally does not mean unconditionally accepting their unloving acts.

for growth, healing, and ascension that they came to bring us. I know that if I hadn't gone through my own traumas, I never would have embarked on the journey I needed to heal them nor learned the lessons of self-love, respect, worth, and empowerment that I did from them. I may never have ended up becoming a coach and healer myself and would likely not be writing this very book to serve you and your fellow sisters.

Finally, Kuan Yin asks that above all, you always offer the gift of compassion and forgiveness to yourself. Be kind in all that you think and say to yourself, beloved. Practice what the Buddhists call *metta*, or loving-kindness, with yourself in every moment. You are doing the best you can. You always have and always will.

Forgive yourself for any mistakes you think you have made. Release the unkind emotions of guilt and self-blame, and replace them with self-compassion and forgiveness. Learn from past mistakes and make more conscious and loving choices in the future. But let go of everything else as it is not who you are. You are a Divine, perfect child of the Universe, and a Goddess of mercy and grace.

Come now, my sister, and let Kuan Yin wash away all your suffering with Her healing waters, and purify your heart through the power of forgiveness. Because *you deserve to be free.*

Pre-Initiation Preparation:

- Play a chant of the Kuan Yin mantra, *"Om Mane Pad- me Hum"* (you can easily find beautiful renditions on YouTube, iTunes, etc.) softly in the background.

- Place a bowl of spring water on your altar.

- Light a white or pink candle.

- Burn incense (use lotus if you can find it).

Kuan Yin's Initiation: Rising as the Lotus
Ritual Type: Guided Meditation

Sit in easy pose (legs crossed), or place your left foot on your right thigh to activate more yin/feminine energy.

If you feel called to do so, open your meditation in prayer pose, with palms of hands touching, and chant Kuan Yin's other mantra, *"Namo Kuan Shi Yin Pusa"* three times.

Lift your right hand up beside your right breast, and bring the tips of your right thumb and index finger together. Rest your left hand on your lap, with the tips of your thumb and index finger touching as well. (If your right arm gets tired during the meditation, simply rest it on your lap. Place your right palm up, and rest your left hand over it with the palm also facing up, tips of the thumbs gently touching).

Closing your eyes, take a few deep breaths into your heart space. If it helps, keep silently chanting "*Namo Kuan Shi Yin Pusa*" to connect with the Goddess's energy.

Feel or see Kuan Yin slowly appear before you, shining with a soft pink glow and floating on a beautiful pink lotus flower.

She sweetly welcomes you to sit on Her lap and takes you into Her all-encompassing embrace. Slowly, She lifts you into the inner realms where you find yourself floating with Her over a dark, murky pond.

As you look down at the muddy water, each passing wave reveals painful events from which you still harbor grief, anger, resentment, judgment, bitterness, or anything else that still feels heavy and painful. As you witness each act, you let any remaining tears and rage to flow forth, and Kuan Yin gently washes them with *amrita* (holy water)— which She carries in a sacred vase.

Go ahead and share anything that you need to with Her—all your sadness and suffering—and allow Her to ceaselessly pour Her *amrita* waters to cleanse and purify you. There is nothing you have to do here, beloved, but invite Kuan Yin's healing love.

Where your heart resists, She opens the way for forgiveness and release. Now, affirm before Her:

In the power of this holy moment, I now release all pain

from past experiences for complete healing, purification, and transmutation. I ask that all karma created between us (your perpetrators) be forgiven, healed, and cleared for everyone involved, without exception, for everyone's best and highest good. I keep only the lessons and growth, and surrender everything else to the Divine. Let there be nothing unfinished between us. I set them free, and I am free.

If you feel the need to do this with specific people, Kuan Yin calls in their higher selves—their pure, wise, loving, and eternal souls—that you may affirm this statement individually with each person. Imagine them coming and leaving in bubbles of light as you call in and then set each soul free.

Finally, turn your gaze lovingly inward, and forgive yourself. Forgive all effects of all past mistakes with grace and compassion.

When you are done, Kuan Yin pours Her *amrita* into the pond, instantly transforming it into a pool of clear, glistening water.

Each glowing wave now illuminates a higher, spiritual lesson behind each experience you have just released:

- The victimhood that initiates the lesson of empowerment.

- The neglect that initiates the lesson of self-love.

- The abandonment that initiates the lesson of self-value.

- The betrayal that initiates the lesson of discernment.

- The heartbreak that initiates the lesson of worthiness.

- The loss that initiates the lesson of faith.

- The abuse that initiates the lesson of self-respect.

Wave upon wave, you now open to your spirit's highest capacity to receive the sacred and invaluable lessons every experience has brought you so that you may rise above the pain and transcend into a Goddess of wisdom and compassion yourself.

As you invite the grace of each lesson, it flourishes into a new lotus flower. They start blooming all around you until you are surrounded by a pond of heavenly lotuses.

You turn softly to Kuan Yin, who radiates Her unconditional love, compassion, and wisdom through you, opening your mind, heart, body, and spirit to receive Her gifts fully and completely.

She gently floats you back into your room now where you reconnect with your body through your breath. She blesses your bowl of water, transforming it into Her holy *amrita*.

Coming out of your meditation with palms pressing together into your heart, you bow down to yourself and Kuan Yin with reverence.

You may now take the bowl of water and sprinkle the holy gift from Kuan Yin all over yourself in blessing.

Anoint all your *chakras* with it too (located at your crown, forehead, throat, heart, stomach, womb, and pubic bone).

Celebrate the bliss of freedom you have just attained through the healing waters of forgiveness. It is safe for you to flow forward and flourish, rising with the pure beauty and grace of a freshly bloomed lotus.

POST-INITIATION SELF-CARE:

- Drink a lot of fresh spring water afterward.

- Journal about your feelings and anything else you need to release.

- Write your lessons on a separate page, and meditate with Kuan Yin on how to apply these lessons.

- Chant the Kuan Yin mantras anytime you need to find grace, compassion, or forgiveness.

AFFIRMING KUAN YIN:

I hold you always in my heart.
I heal you with my *amrita*.

Your tears and prayers are in my care.
For I live in your bliss and your despair.

I Am Kuan Yin.

Goddess Kuan Yin

Origin: East Asian

Also Called: Guan Yin, Guanyin, Kwun Yam, Kun Iam, Kuan Im, Kannon, Kanzeon, Kuan Yin Medaw, Chenrezik, Kab Yeeb

Name Meaning: Goddess of mercy

Attributes:

- Mercy
- Compassion
- Forgiveness
- Grace
- Healing
- Miracles
- Transcendence
- Spirituality
- Loving-kindness
- Wisdom
- Meditation

Sacred Symbols:

- Lotus
- *Amrita* (holy water)
- Vase
- Ponds
- Willow branch
- Lotus incense
- Flowing robes

Chakras:

- Heart
- Third eye
- Crown

Element: Water

Essential Oils:

- Lotus
- White rose
- German chamomile
- Sandalwood

Colors:

- White
- Pink
- Purple
- Red

Crystals:

- Rose quartz
- Jade
- Emerald
- Pink tourmaline

Archetype in Balance:

- Compassionate
- Understanding
- Patient
- Helpful
- Thoughtful
- Loving
- Kind
- Considerate

- Nurturing

Archetype out of Balance:

- Over-giving
- Martyr
- Resentful
- Bitter
- Passive

- Overly compromising
- Lacks boundaries
- Lacks balance of giving and receiving
- Tries to rescue others

Creating Balance:

- Practice the *metta* (loving-kindness) meditation by wishing all beings (including yourself) peace and freedom from suffering.

- Be compassionate with yourself.

- Heal your heart through forgiveness.

- Speak up to or let go of those who mistreat you.

- Free yourself of toxic emotional patterns.

- Empower others to help themselves instead of taking on their issues.

- Rise above challenges with wisdom and grace.

- Keep your heart open to love.

- Give and receive in balance.

- Ask for help and accept it.

- Have faith that your prayers are always heard and answered, sometimes in unexpected, but always benevolent, ways.

- Open yourself to miracles.

- Be a channel of love and peace.

- Only do what you can from love, not obligation or guilt.

Associated Goddesses:

- Mother Mary (Christian)

- White Buffalo Calf Woman (Native American)

- White Tara (Tibetan)

- Isis (Egyptian)

Prayer/Invocation:

Beloved Kuan Yin, as the Goddess of compassion within me, please cleanse and heal my heart of all past pain that still resides within me. Wash away all my sorrows with your holy amrita *waters so that my heart may arise and unfold as pure as your fully blossomed lotus flower.*

Bring me the grace of forgiveness so that I may be free to live and love openly, deeply, and joyfully. I receive your miraculous healing now. Namo Kuan Shi Yin Pusa. So be it. So it is.

Gateway 6

Embracing Divine Love, Pleasure, and Joy

Initiator:
Aphrodite, Goddess of Love

Aphrodite

LET MY WORSHIP BE WITHIN
THE HEART THAT REJOICES, FOR
BEHOLD, ALL ACTS OF LOVE AND
PLEASURE ARE MY RITUALS.
—DOREEN VALIENTE, "CHARGE OF THE
GODDESS"

Beloved, as you arrive here gently but powerfully cleansed of all that was not serving you with the grace of the Goddesses you have awakened thus far, I hope you can feel the floodgates of your Divine nectar ready to erupt forth. For as you have bravely purged all that is not truly you, you are now going to reclaim and unleash all that is. And you are going to relish in this luscious, blissful re-birthing gloriously and boldly as is only befitting to your next initiatory Goddess: Aphrodite.

It is essential to tap into Her now, because She will fill the space you have created by releasing your pain with love and delight. As a Goddess without a childhood, Aphrodite requires that we heal our past wounds before we are ready to embrace Her. When we have done our part to clear the old, She will gladly meet us, replenishing and reigniting us with the self-worth and value required to begin to co-create the life we desire and deserve.

When we are disconnected from our Aphrodite nature, every part of our life reflects this. No matter how hard we try, we are constantly met with blocks and frustrations. As I learned so painfully on my own journey and witness with my clients, a deep (often unconscious) void of self-love gets mirrored back to us with people and situations that don't love and respect us either. In relationships, our insecurity makes us needy and clingy or distant and aloof, pushing away the very people we want to be closer to. At worst, a lack of self-love makes us want to hold on to people who are toxic for us.

In all our relationships, we continue to crave love and fear true intimacy. Intimacy requires vulnerability, and vulnerability can be terrifying when we haven't yet cultivated our inner Aphrodite—when we lack self-love. Because to make ourselves vulnerable opens us up to the possibility of getting hurt, betrayed, rejected, or abandoned. On a deeper level, we fear becoming vulnerable because such painful experiences would reinforce a much deeper fear: that we are unlovable, unworthy, and undeserving; that we are inherently not good enough.

Since we don't feel good enough, we compensate by attempting to earn love, approval, and affection by over-giving our energy, resources, talents, time, and—especially connected to Aphrodite—our hearts and bodies. We might seek people who need us, people whom we can heal, support, and "fix," so that we can guilt, obligate, and indebt them into staying with us.

In doing so, we create and perpetuate cycles of unbalanced and disempowering relationships instead of the fulfilling and honoring ones we deserve. Beyond relationships, when we are disconnected from our Aphrodite nature, we don't allow ourselves to own our desires, nor do we know how to attract or receive them.

No more, beloved!

You have already done such deep and difficult work with the previous Goddesses. Aphrodite is here at this sacred juncture to propel you on a new path: one of sacred love, pleasure, and joy.

As Greek Goddess of self, romantic, sexual, and Divine love, Aphrodite is here to remind you that love in all its forms is not only your Divine birthright, but your inherent nature. Love is *who you are*. It is what you are made of. It is where and what you come from. It is where and what you return to. It is what you are here to be. It is how you are meant to live. It is what you are here to give and receive in abundant and ecstatic flow.

She is the part of you that knows that you are not only intrinsically worthy of life's sweetest gifts, but that as the perfect manifestation of Divine love:

Love in all its forms is not only your Divine birthright, but your inherent nature. Love is who you are.

- *You* are the embodiment of beauty.

- *You* are the gateway to ecstasy.

- *You* are the generator of joy.

- *You* are the source of vitality.

- *You* are the flow of prosperity.

- *You* are the expansion of desire.

- *You* are the muse of inspiration.

- *You* are the womb of fertility.

- *You* are the vessel of creativity.

- *You* are the lover and the beloved.

Aphrodite sees only your true nature, and She is here to help you see it too. For She knows that there is a Goddess of love waiting to emerge through you, and it is Aphrodite's sacred honor to midwife her birth.

While Her origins connect back to more ancient Goddesses like Ishtar, Inanna, and Isis, Aphrodite's classical Greek origin story establishes a fertile foundation for reconnecting with your own love goddess nature. According to Hesiod's version, She was born of the foam that erupted from the sea when Greek God Cronus cut off His father Uranus's genitals and threw His castrated phallus into the tumultuous Aegean Sea. As water and semen merged, Aphrodite erupted as a fully grown Goddess, nude, whole, and most beautiful—ready to love and be loved.

When you love yourself fully enough to be open to all experiences, you become, like Aphrodite, a vessel for love, beauty, and bliss.

Her natural nudity and immediate receptivity to love reminds us that if we desire love, we must be willing to "bare it all." We must be ready to be pure in heart and nude in spirit, revealing and being ourselves completely. We must show up in our full, vulnerable glory, trusting that the infinite abode of love within us will heal and overcome any lack of love we experience with others.

Awakening Aphrodite within you in this way is about knowing that you have the capacity to love yourself through anything, and that others' acts will never diminish your inherent nature as a Goddess of love. When you love yourself fully enough to be open to all experiences, you become, like Aphrodite, a vessel for love, beauty, and bliss.

Upon Her birth, Aphrodite was greeted by the seasons who first adorned Her heavenly body and then whisked Her away to Her eventual home on earth—the island of Cyprus. Wherever She stepped, sweet grass grew and flowers bloomed. Roses are said to have appeared on earth at Her birth. Wild animals ceased their preying and started mating in Her presence. Every place She graced, Aphrodite inspired laughter, beauty, love, and joy. Her essence seems perfectly captured in the poem, "An Interlude," by Algernon Charles Swinburne:

You came, and the sun came after,
And the green grass grew golden above;
And the flag-flowers lightened with laughter,
And the meadow-sweet shook with love.

Aphrodite was unique in the pantheon of Greek Goddesses. She loved love, pleasure, and sex, but—like the virgin Goddesses Athena (Goddess of wisdom and war), Artemis (Goddess of the wild, hunt, and moon), Hestia (Goddess of home and hearth), and Hecate (Goddess of magic and protection), She valued and required Her autonomy. She maintained Her independence even as She was wife to the blacksmith God Hephaestus and mothered several children from different Gods. She did what pleased Her freely and unapologetically.

Even as the Goddess who stirred rapture and desire, no male—Divine or mortal—ever dared to touch Aphrodite without Her consent, unlike the tragic rapes suffered by Hera (Queen of heaven) from Zeus (King of Gods), Demeter (Goddess of harvest) from Poseidon (God of sea), and Persephone (Goddess of spring and Queen of the underworld) by Hades (God of the underworld).

While these three Goddesses eventually healed from their violations, they were not accorded the honor and respect they deserved and were subjugated to the will of male Gods (the rapes represented the rise of patriarchy and its degradation of the Goddess and women during Greece's Classical era). As a traditionalist determined to preserve Her honor, Hera decided to marry Zeus, and their tumultuous marriage was marked by His affairs and Her attempts at revenge. Persephone was, by many accounts, tricked into marrying Hades, whom She spent the six months of fall and winter with each year until She reunited with Her mother Demeter to create spring and summer.

While the Divine position of these Goddesses was undermined and/or determined by the male Gods, Aphrodite's status as Goddess of love was one no one dared to threaten. In this way, Aphrodite manages to stand apart from both the virgin and "victim" Goddesses. She enjoys the freedom of the virgin Goddesses and is spared the fate of the more vulnerable Goddesses. She relishes in life's joys and pleasures on Her own terms and to Her heart's content, knowing that it is safe and right for Her to do so.

ACTIVATING SACRED SELF-LOVE

Aphrodite's gift to every woman is this very sacred reminder: that you are worthy of self, romantic, and Divine love, as you are the very source of love itself.

When activating Her gifts of self-love, Aphrodite requires you to love every part of yourself unconditionally. She asks that you speak only lovingly to yourself. She asks that you treat yourself with the deepest love and

You are worthy of self, romantic, and Divine love as you are the very source of love itself.

reverence. She asks that you expect others to treat you lovingly, as you treat them lovingly, too. She asks that you practice sacred self-care and nourish your mind, body, and spirit with beautiful, loving thoughts and actions. She asks that you see yourself as She does—through the eyes of love.

LOVING YOUR BODY TEMPLE

She especially asks that you have complete acceptance and adoration of your body temple, which is Her sacred abode. Yet She knows that for many of us women, body love can be a very challenging feat, given the impossible standards and extreme expectations set by our society on feminine beauty.

Yet no matter what the expectations of others, Aphrodite upholds herself to only one's standards: her own. When She looks at Herself, fellow women, and all people, She sees only our Divine radiance and beauty, through and through. She asks that you cease looking for "flaws" and things you wish to "fix," and instead embrace the body you already inhabit as perfectly beautiful and inherently holy, beloved.

If, on top of cultural pressures, you have experienced abuse of any form (especially sexual), then I know firsthand how much more difficult learning to love and honor ourselves and our bodies can be. Any violation we experience creates a deep wound on a physical, emotional, psychological, and energetic level. That is why our work with the previous Goddesses was so essential. And yet, if you haven't already, please consider getting further support to heal from any abuse you have experienced, beloved, as I know this can be a deep and intense journey requiring professional help.

What Aphrodite can help you with right now, sweet sister, is gently and powerfully reconnecting you to the source of love already within you. While She inhabits your entire body temple, Aphrodite specifically embodies your *yoni* and heart. *Yoni* is the Sanskrit word for "vagina" or "womb," but it actually translates to "abode" and "source." It is both the cause and gateway of Divine pleasure, orgasmic joy, and ecstatic creativity within you.

Energetically, Aphrodite resides in your *yoni* at your sacral *chakra* (below your navel), and in your heart *chakra*, at the center of your beautiful breasts.

When you re-awaken Her essence in these sacred centers, you unleash the gifts of love, passion, joy, sensuality, creativity, fertility, and even prosperity in your life. You claim your desires as sacred and know that you are worthy of their fullest expression and enjoyment.

Honoring Your Sexuality as Sacred

One of the greatest gifts Aphrodite awakens through Her *chakras* is aligning our sexuality with our hearts. By awakening the sacral *chakra*, She empowers us to love and honor our bodies, own our desire for sexual union (with ourselves or others), and claim our worthiness for orgasmic pleasure. She reminds you that your sexuality is sacred and you deserve to honor it.

If She were only to reside in the sexual *chakra*, however, we could misuse Her power and deny ourselves the love and respect (that She Herself demanded) that we deserve when sharing our bodies with another.

By awakening through our hearts, Aphrodite alchemizes self-love with sexual desire. Aphrodite never had sex with anyone in exchange for their love and loyalty. She was first and foremost loyal to Herself and commanded that anyone (mortal or God) who wished the privilege of making love to Her be worthy and honoring of Her Goddess nature.

She freely chose Her many lovers, and She chose only those who revered and ravished her. She teaches us that in order to enjoy the fullest expression of our sexuality, we must first be fully connected to our own sacred self-worth.

By awakening through our hearts and yonis, Aphrodite alchemizes self-love with sexual desire.

As beautifully expressed in the following verse from the neo-pagan text, "Charge of the Goddess," Aphrodite wants us to be free to enjoy our bodies and all of life's pleasures with reverence and love:

"And as a sign that ye be truly free,
you shall be naked in your rites;
and ye shall dance, sing, feast, make music and love,
all in my praise.

For mine is the ecstasy of the spirit,
and mine also is joy on earth;
for my law is love unto all beings."

—Doreen Valiente

Where male-dominated religions perverted physical, sexual, and earthly pleasure with sin, shame, and guilt—making you feel bad for feeling good—Goddess traditions honor pleasure as sacred and natural. They know that when you feel good, you feel the Goddess.

Because the essence of the Divine is love and joy, when you experience these exalted states, you have a direct experience of the Divine, specifically the Divine Feminine. Aphrodite as the Goddess of both Divine love and pleasure is the very essence of this embodied within *you.*

Your body temple is the vessel to experience the Sacred Feminine gifts of pleasure through your senses and your soul, without guilt or apology.

Owning Your Desires

When you awaken Aphrodite in your sacral and heart *chakras* and entire body temple, you will unleash the luscious power of your sacred desires. You will feel turned on to life. It is vital that you allow yourself to own and honor your true desires and have the self-awareness to know exactly what you are wanting and why. Because Aphrodite knows that when we are disconnected from the inner desires behind our outer desires, we may attempt to fill them with things that won't in fact satisfy us. She asks that whenever you seek to fulfill a desire, you ask yourself what you really, truly desire:

- Do you desire sex or to feel more connected?

- Do you desire a romantic partner or to feel more loved?

- Do you desire ice cream or to feel more supported?

- Do you desire that new dress or to feel more beautiful?

- Do you desire that designer bag or to feel more worthy?

- Do you desire the big house or to feel more secure?

- Do you desire more money or to feel free?

All your desires—be they external or internal—are Divine and worthy, and you are Divinely worthy of their highest, most joyous fulfillment. Aphrodite simply asks that you know yourself and know what you desire beneath your desires. Once you are clear on this, as the muse Goddess, Aphrodite Herself will inspire you to find the most joyous and loving path to honoring your desires.

ACTIVATING APHRODITE

As you cultivate Aphrodite by unleashing the source of love and joy within you, you become irresistible to life's blessings and delight in all its pleasures. You fall in love with yourself and your life and feel adored by life itself. Everything and everyone around you is ignited by your radiance and uplifted by your presence. You laugh easily and often. You feel a deep sense of richness, beauty, and fulfillment. You love and honor your body, and your body returns this love with health and vitality. You feel inspired to live fully and passionately, and inspire others to do so too. Your passion becomes contagious, your joy becomes infectious.

Your self-love remains rooted in Divine love and makes you magnetic to the highest form of romantic or soulmate

When you feel good, you feel the Goddess.

love if you desire it. Eventually, you become a clear and potent vessel of infinite love and become, like Aphrodite, a Goddess of love yourself.

It is time now to invite Aphrodite in, beloved, so that She may re-initiate you into your true origin and essence of pure joy and infinite love.

The sacred initiation below is inspired by Aphrodite's own yearly renewal, in which She returns to her homeland of Cyprus each spring to bathe in Her sacred waters and renew Her virginity. As Her maidens adorn Her upon Her rise from the sea, Aphrodite emerges even more beautiful and joyous, and ever more ready to experience the fullness of Her own Divine nature.

PRE-INITIATION PREPARATION:

Aphrodite's Sacred Bath

Transform your bathroom into Aphrodite's sanctuary however you feel guided, or try the below tips.

If you have a bathtub:

- Add rose/flower petals, sea salt, and essential oils (especially myrrh and rose), to your bath water (provided it is safe for you to use essential oils).

- Drop a tumbled rose quartz crystal into your bath water.

If you have/prefer a shower:

- Make a shower scrub with fine sea salt, light olive or coconut oil, and essential oils of your choice (see suggestions above).

- Place the rose quartz crystal near you.

In your bathroom:

- (Safely) add incense, candles, and seashells, or any other items that represent beauty and love to you around your bath.

- Play relaxation music (ocean waves is ideal) softly in the background.

Safety first:

- With either the bath or shower option, make sure you are not too tired or taking any drowsy medications, and avoid alcohol before/after.

- Set up a timer for 15–20 minutes to avoid being in your bath/shower for too long.

- If it's not safe or comfortable for you to bathe in water for this ritual, simply sit or lie in meditation at your altar and visualize the journey below.

Post-bath items:

- Create a post-bath Goddess kit with a luxurious body oil (add essential oil to any carrier oil like coconut), strawberries and chocolate, sensual music, and a soft, flowing nightgown or even lingerie.

APHRODITE'S INITIATION: EMBRACING DIVINE LOVE, PLEASURE, AND JOY
Ritual Type: Bath/Shower Guided Meditation, or Guided Meditation only

Enter the sanctuary of your bathroom.

Play your relaxation music (ocean waves are great for this part). Light your incense and candles. Prepare anything else you need to (like adding things to your bath).

Slowly undress yourself with intention.

Take a moment to pause outside of your bath/shower, and place your left hand on your *yoni* (sacral *chakra*) by pressing your palm just above your pubic bone, your fingers reaching towards your *yoni*. Place your other hand on or between your breasts to touch your heart *chakra*.

Welcome Aphrodite to join you with a heart-prayer, or say this one:

Beloved Aphrodite, Golden Goddess of all love, beauty, and bliss, I welcome you now into the sacred temple of my space, my body, and my heart. I have come a long way. I have released so much. I now ask for your love and blessing so that you may restore, renew, and re-plenish me as you yourself did each spring. Revitalize and re-ignite me so that I too may be reconnected to the infinite flow of love in all its forms, on every level, in every part of my life. I am open to receiving all your love and support now. Thank you. So be it.

If taking a bath:

Slowly step into your bath and get comfortable.

Enjoy the feeling of being immersed in these sacred waters. Keep your head above the water and rest it on the support behind you (tub/wall/cushion).

If taking a shower:

After stepping into your shower, start gently massaging your sea salt scrub all over your body.

After turning the water to a comfortable tempera-ture, sit or lie on the floor of the shower so that the water pours over your body.

APHRODITE SACRED BATH VISUALIZATION:

Close your eyes if it is safe for you to do so.

Imagine yourself being transported to Aphrodite's

home island of Cyprus, where She greets you with Her lovely maidens. They welcome you into the playful waves of the Aegean Sea. They ask you to float here as they safely hold you up.

They now flow wave upon wave of these primal waters over your entire body. The water is filled with foamy white light, and this light flows through your entire being.

Aphrodite now directs the water to flow even more powerfully through your *yoni*—into every dark and Divine part of your feminine center—and into your heart—the sacred abode of infinite love.

The healing light of these holy waters washes away any remaining energetic, psychic, physical, emotional, mental, karmic, and unconscious residue of past experiences. They cleanse away all words, actions, and events that harmed your body and heart in any way. They clear away all pains and patterns of heartbreak, rejection, self-denial, self-criticism, all shame and guilt, all fear of punishment, and all resistance to receiving your due good. There is nothing you have to do here but let go and allow in this healing while remaining physically aware and present. If there are any memories, emotions, or tears that come up, let them flow out of you gently, surrendering them to the Goddess of love.

You can silently affirm any specific experiences, patterns, or blocks around love and joy that you are releasing.

Once you have surrendered everything you need to, Aphrodite magically changes the color of Her light-filled waters to a soft, beautiful pink and golden orange. She allows these waters to flow into your entire being to replenish you now with the sacred blessings of love and bliss.

The golden orange light swirls through your sacral *chakra* as the pink light ignites your heart. Both lights fill and overflow from your entire body temple as you radiate with Divine love, pleasure, and joy.

You feel this love and bliss—the very essence of your own Divine nature—awaken and permeate through you. It radiates out to your body, heart, and mind. It expands out to your entire soul. It expands further to all those you love. It expands to those who have hurt you. It expands to everyone you know. It expands to everyone on earth. It expands to all beings everywhere—uplifting all with your own Divine radiance. You are this powerful. You are this vessel.

Now see and feel all the light and love of the entire universe flowing back to you, manifold. Receive it all into your body, heart, and being where Aphrodite both seals and unleashes it.

You have now been cleansed, purified, and renewed in Aphrodite's sacred waters by the Goddess Herself. You are ready to emerge whole, rebirthed, and radiant—as a Goddess yourself.

She and Her maidens now help you come back and

step out of the ocean and onto Her sacred shore. They adorn you with beautiful clothes, perfume, and jewels and offer you sweet treats to delight in. Together, they honor your rebirth with a celebratory dance as you relish in being a woman and re-emerging as a Goddess.

Through this dance, you bring your awareness fully into your body and back into your bathroom. Open your eyes. Thank Aphrodite. Take your time getting up.

Drain your tub if taking a bath, and shower off any remaining sea salt and oil before slowly stepping outside.

Use your fresh towels or bathrobe to dry off, and then stay nude for post-initiation self-care, or get dressed if you need to complete now.

Put out all candles/incense unless you are ready for the post-initiation rituals. If so, move your sacred objects into your bedroom or altar space.

Post-Initiation Self-Care:

- After your bath/shower, enter the sanctuary of your altar or bedroom.

- Play sensual music in the background.

- Slowly and sensually, massage your body oil all over yourself, working towards your heart. Focus especially on your hips, thighs, womb, and heart.

- Slide on your nightgown or lingerie.

- Ground yourself by sensuously savoring your sweet treats, such as strawberries and dark chocolate.

- As you relish in these delights, affirm silently or aloud, new love-centered truths. Let your heart and body guide you as to what these are. You can say statements like, *"I allow myself to receive. It is safe for me to enjoy. It is sacred for me to be joy. I am love. I am loved. I am a Goddess of love. I am beautiful. I love myself."*

- Now start dancing to your chosen music to seal in and embody Aphrodite's blessed initiation.

- Allow yourself to fill up with delight and daydream of fresh new desires that spring from your heart and womb, which will come to be with ease, grace, and joy—like the flow of your ecstatic dance.

Affirming Aphrodite

My body is my temple
The very vessel of bliss.

I am an ocean of endless pleasures
Flow in my sweet abyss.

I Am Aphrodite.

Goddess Aphrodite

Origin: Greek

Name Meaning: Foam born

Attributes:

- Love
- Sensuality
- Sexuality
- Pleasure
- Joy
- Desire
- Beauty
- Fun

- Fertility
- Muse/inspiration
- Laughter
- Music
- Dance
- Flourishing
- Radiance

Sacred Symbols:

- Sea/water
- Roses
- Scallop shells
- White dove
- Chalice

- Myrrh
- Perfumes and oils
- Golden girdle
- Gold coins
- Swan

- Dove
- Incense
- Apple

- Pomegranate
- Meadows
- Red anemone flowers

Chakras:

- Heart
- Sacral

Element: Water

Essential Oils:

- Rose
- Myrrh
- Patchouli
- Ylang-ylang

Colors:

- White
- Pink
- Orange-gold
- Gold
- Green

Crystals:

- Rose quartz
- Emerald
- Carnelian

Archetype in Balance:

- Loving
- Joyful
- Sensual
- Confident
- Creates and appreciates beauty
- Inspired and inspiring
- Artistic
- Radiant
- Receptive
- Magnetic
- Charismatic

- Exuberant
- Laughs easily
- Grounded
- Sensitive
- Sexually empowered
- Honors body as temple
- Embraces natural beauty and aging process
- Values inner and outer beauty in balance
- Feels beautiful from the inside out
- Loves self and others

Archetype out of Balance:

- Hedonistic
- Selfish
- Vain
- Superficial
- Materialistic

- Promiscuous
- Stifled
- Unfaithful
- Flaky
- Frigid

- Insecure

- Codependent relationships

- Compromises self to please others, especially love interests

- Feels incomplete without a romantic partner

- Fears rejection and abandonment

- Resents children or responsibilities that get in the way of dating, partying, shopping, and/or indulging

- Lacks clarity or discipline to act on inspired ideas

- Irresponsible with money

- Uses body, sex, and beauty as currency

- Resists/resents aging process

- Greedy

- Gossip

- Jealous

- Competitive (especially for attention and men)

- Addiction-prone

Creating Balance:

- Have and practice sacred self-love.

- Heal your relationship with yourself.

- Heal your childhood wounds so you can be a secure, happy, confident woman.

- Value yourself outside of your relationships.

- Love your life now.

- Release guilt and enjoy what brings you pleasure.

- Honor your body in every way: what you eat, how you move, what you wear, who can touch you and how.

- Do what brings you joy.

- Release guilt about receiving.

- Affirm your Divine self-worth.

- Laugh often.

- Dance more.

- Take sea salt baths, or bathe in the sea/ocean.

- Live more from your senses.

- Fully appreciate the smell, touch, taste, sound, and sight of everyday experiences.

- Embrace your sexuality as natural, beautiful, and sacred.

- Be present in lovemaking.

- Practice sacred self-care rituals to help you feel more sensual, relaxed, and Goddessy.

- Allow yourself to be vulnerable, to share your true self.

- Get to the root of your deeper desires beneath cravings.

- Take joyful measures to fulfill your deeper desires for love, affection, intimacy, connection, appreciation, support, understanding, etc.

- Share your desires and needs with others.

- Allow yourself to open up and be vulnerable to create intimacy in relationships.

- Be generous with yourself and others.

- Avoid overspending and overindulging.

- Live within your means.

- Create more beauty in your environment.

- Eat and enjoy delicious food.

- Spend more time in nature.

- Read poetry, watch romantic movies, and/or visit an art gallery.

- Commit to "me time" and create "me dates."

- Release energetic attachments to past lovers through visualization and Aphrodite baths with sea salt.

- Explore sacred sexuality practices (such as Tantra and Kama Sutra).

- Get gentle touch therapies (massages, Reiki) from a licensed professional you feel safe with to help clear energetic blocks and balance your *chakras*.

Associated Goddesses:

- Venus (Roman)

- Freya (Norse)

- Lalita Devi (Indian)

- Lilith (Mesopotamian)

- Hathor (Egyptian)

- Lakshmi (Indian)

- Abundantia (Roman)

Prayer/Invocation:

Beloved Aphrodite, as Goddess of love within me, open me now to the delights of my body temple. I now release all shame and guilt around experiencing my Goddess-given gifts and rights of sacred pleasure and joy.

Ensure that I treat myself and my body with reverence. Help me to see myself through your eyes, seeing all my Divine beauty and perfection. Help me to love, appreciate, and adore every part of myself, as well as others, while ensuring that I am treated with love and respect.

Help me to know that I am love embodied. Let me radiate Divine love and joy out in blessing to all, and let me be open to experiencing love in all its blessed forms. So be it. So it is.

Gateway 7

SETTING YOUR SIGHTS TO THE STARS

INITIATOR:
TARA, GODDESS OF WISHES

Tara

...WAIT FOR THE CLOUDS TO CLEAR, AND YOU'LL SEE YOUR DESTINY SHINING AS BRIGHTLY AS EVER: THE FIXED POINT IN THE CONSTANTLY CHANGING CONSTELLATIONS OF YOUR LIFE.
—MARTHA BECK

I hope you are fresh from relishing in your Aphrodisian initiation, beloved, filled and overflowing with love, pleasure, and joy. As you have now purged, healed, and transformed what no longer serves you and arrived here whole and blissfully radiant, you are primed to align your deepest desires with your divine destiny. Initiating you on this flight is the celestial Goddess, Tara.

While as a Hindu and Buddhist Goddess, Tara is intertwined with Avalokiteshvara and Kuan Yin, She maintains Her own identity outside of this association and is worshiped in Her own right as the Swift Savioress. Her name has several meanings, including, "the one who ferries across," "star," and "she who grants wishes."

Tara is the benevolent ally who carries us through each stage of our lives with courage, grace, and wisdom. She is

Tara is the ever-shining star who invites you to set your aspirations heaven high, like the brilliant stars scattered across the midnight sky.

the liberator who frees us from being small versions of our unlimited selves. She is the ever-shining star who invites us to set our aspirations heaven high, like the brilliant stars scattered across the midnight sky.

She is the muse who inspires the co-creation of our dreams with graceful surrender, just as She sits on Her fully bloomed lotus flower. And, should we ask, She is ever ready to illuminate every part of our journey and grant wishes along the way.

As a multi-functioning Goddess, Tara has twenty-one main aspects, which are represented by Her various colors. Her most venerated forms are:

White Tara: Grants wishes, removes obstacles, bestows longevity, emanates rays of light, provides peace and healing, teaches *mudras* (sacred hand gestures), inspires creativity, and destroys poison (including toxic inner conditions).

Green Tara: Mother of the Buddhas, Swift Savioress, grants wishes, provides refuge, bringer of wisdom and enlightenment. She is also invoked with Her mantra, *"Om Tara Tuttare Ture Soha"* to protect against eight specific outer and inner calamities:

1. Lions/Pride

2. Wild elephants/Delusion and ignorance

3. Fire/Hatred

4. Snakes/Envy

5. Robbers/Fanatical views

6. Imprisonment/Greed

7. Floods/Attachment

8. Demons/Fear and Doubt

Black Tara: Sacred wrath, provides ultimate protection, Goddess of power.

Yellow Tara: Provides prosperity and success.

Blue Tara: Simultaneous seer of past, present, and future, transmutes anger, aids with meditation, concentration, discipline, patience, and effort.

Red Tara: Helps with harsh but necessary transformations as well as with attracting and manifesting.

Through Her various roles, Tara acts as the Divine Mother who wants what is best for Her beloved children. She reminds you that you are worthy of your wishes, and that She stands ready to help you manifest them.

She asks you to look beyond what has been and what you may see around you even right now that does not match your soul's deepest desires and truest capabilities. She wants to ferry you above and beyond what you think you want, what you deem to be possible for you, and align your vision with heaven's highest will for you. She wants to grant you all the inner and outer resources you need to fulfill your Divine destiny.

As Aphrodite has just awakened the seat of your sacred pleasure and joy and centered you in the self-love required to dream big, Tara is here to help you get crystal clear on what to dream of. As women, we often limit what we can conceive to be possible for ourselves because we may not feel worthy of high aspirations *within* ourselves:

We may allow our fears of inadequacy, failure, or uncertainty to hold us back from embracing and living our greatest potential.

We may lack faith that the universe will do its part should we summon the courage to do ours in the direction of our dreams.

We may play small to let others shine.

We may hesitate to get what we want out of fear of taking someone else's share—of light, love, success, wealth, happiness, support, and/or brilliance.

We may feel that we need permission from a source outside of ourselves to fully commit to our dreams.

These and many other inner, hidden saboteurs are the reasons we journeyed with the previous Goddesses. We needed to ensure that by the time you meet Tara, you have freed yourself of these debilitating inner blocks, so that you are ready to receive Her support in aligning with what you Divinely deserve and are destined for.

Tara is here to help you give yourself permission to dream your greatest dreams. She is here to liberate you from all that may still hold you back. She is here to help you envision and expect the best and brightest present and future for yourself.

She is especially committed to helping us women claim our sacred potential under patriarchal conditions, as She Herself is a powerful advocate for our right to do so. In one of Her origin stories, She was a Buddhist devotee and otherworldly princess whose name meant, "Moon of primordial awareness," or "Moon of wisdom-knowledge."

Her dedicated practice and service led Her to earn special merit and instruction on *bodhicitta* (the aspiration to attain enlightenment and help all sentient beings). Noting Her imminent ascension, a few monks approached Her and suggested that She pray to be born as a male in Her following incarnations in order to reach complete enlightenment.

The wise and empowered princess retorted back—more firmly than gracefully as the matter required—that their very perception that gender is a detriment to one's ability to attain enlightenment is evidence of their provincial and ignorant thinking. As His Holiness the Dalai Lama explains in his book, *The*

Path to Tranquility: Daily Wisdom, after expressing Her fair frustration on the position of the feminine to the monks, Tara declared:

> *"I have developed bodhicitta as a woman. For all my lifetimes along the path I vow to be born as a woman, and in my final lifetime when I attain Buddhahood, then, too, I will be a woman."*

True to Her vow, She continued Her deep meditation for a few more millennia in female form. The power of Her intensive practice helped free many more beings from suffering. Her continued dedication eventually led Her to attain complete enlightenment and after having become a *bodhi* (enlightened being), She evolved into the great Goddess Tara.

She became venerated by male and female followers alike and trail-blazed a path for women to honor their own journeys to achieve their Divine potential. She boldly demonstrated that *all beings*—regardless of gender—are worthy and capable of doing so.

In our world, we women continue to face barriers to being all that we can be. Tara, however, is that enlightened part of ourselves that implores and empowers us to go beyond transcending barriers, to establishing new paradigms and possibilities

> *Tara is a revered feminist deity in a male-led religion who inspires us women to claim our Divine value, own our power, and attain our highest aspirations.*

that can benefit *everyone*. She Herself defied limitations and set Her own course and is worshiped and adored for it the world over.

She is a revered feminist deity in a male-led religion who inspires us women to claim our Divine value, own our power, and attain our highest aspirations.

If you are feeling stuck or lost in any part of your life, Tara is the inner star that will guide you back on your path and light every step along your way, beloved.

It is time now to invoke Her presence so that She may align your sights to the stars and grant your soul's highest wishes.

PRE-INITIATION PREPARATION:

- Light a white candle, along with any other of Tara's colors if you wish (green, yellow, red, black, etc., based on which aspect of Hers you wish to connect with).

- Have your journal and pen handy.

- Light incense.

- Find a chant of Tara's mantra, *"Om Tara Tuttare Ture Soha,"* which means, *"Om* and salutations to She who is the source of all blessings," and play it when you are ready to start your ritual.

- Bring a chair to your altar (you will be sitting on it for meditation).

TARA'S INITIATION:
SETTING YOUR SIGHTS TO THE STARS
Ritual type: Meditation and Journaling

Come and sit on your chair. Take Tara's playful posture, *Lalitasana,* meaning "royal ease," by extending your right leg forward and down, toes touching the floor gracefully. Bring your left leg up on the chair, bending at the knee and bringing the left foot close to your *yoni* or right thigh crease, sole of the foot facing up.

Rest your right hand over your right knee with palm facing forward and fingers down and slightly curved in *Varada mudra* (wish-granting gesture). Bend your left elbow and raise your left hand up beside your left breast. Face your left palm forward with tips of thumb and ring finger touching in *Sharagamana mudra* (protection/refuge-giving gesture). You can rest your hands in your lap if you get tired.

Close your eyes and focus on your breath, silently chanting the Tara mantra, *"Om Tara Tuttare Ture Soha"* to connect more deeply with Her essence.

See yourself sitting on a beautiful lotus flower, floating over a pristine pond. It is night, and the stars above glow on the waters below. As you look up to the stars, you see one star getting brighter and brighter. Like a magical shooting star, it now travels down to you, and instantly Tara appears before you.

Luminescent, She smiles at you and emanates Divine, maternal love into your heart center. She keeps shining beams of silvery light into your entire being until your own inner spark begins to shine through.

She invites you to continue to receive Her light and radiate your own as She drops the eternal question, *"Who am I?"* into your consciousness.

You keep asking, "Who am I?" and notice the answers that flow forth.

At first, they may be connected to your gender, race, religion, and roles. Allow yourself to witness any labels you use to define yourself.

Keep asking, "Who am I?" until you go beyond these worldly confines.

When your answers come to take on a more spiritual nature, continue to ask, "Who am I?" even then.

As you remain open to hearing and knowing the answer, Tara gestures you to glance at your reflection in the water, and you behold the sight of yourself:

You see a beautiful, radiant Goddess glowing before you. Tara tells you that *you* are this Goddess—perfect, whole, and divine.

As you bask in the light of your holy truth, Tara now creates a beautiful, sparkling boat beneath you. Sitting with you, She lifts you up into the heavens where you float serenely among the twinkling stars.

Tara asks you to ask yourself the next question: *"What do I want?"*

As you receive each answer, share it with Tara.

Tara starts pointing out specific stars to you, each representing a different area of your life: relationships, health, career, wealth, spirituality, opportunities— everything that is important to you.

You begin to state your desires in each area without holding back. Ask for anything and everything that you wish. See these stars sparkle back in response to each wish you make upon them.

Now when you feel you have asked for all that you could and wished upon all the stars you want, Tara poses Her next question for you: *What do you want for me?*

By "you," you are asking Tara, your own soul, and the Divine to share their highest, most expansive, blissful, abundant, creative, and loving vision for you.

Keep asking, "What do you want for me?"

You look back at Tara's stars—the ones you made wishes upon—and see what the Divine, your higher self, and Tara wished for you on each one in every part of your life. As you scan each star, notice any changes to what the Divine wants for you from what you wished for yourself.

Allow the Divine to show you the highest possibilities and potentials available to you in all areas. Go beyond the areas of your life as the Divine shows even greater, bigger stars that reveal your soul's grand purpose.

You now witness your spirit's highest aspirations. These are not so much dreams as they are sacred visions of what you are truly capable and worthy of as the Divine sees so.

Stay open to any and all visions being revealed to you.

As you notice any doubts or fears arise, Tara morphs into protection mode and begins to liberate you of these fears with Her loving strength. You hold compassion for all these sacred parts of yourself as Tara gently but swiftly frees you of any illusions.

As you look to the stars with peace and trust, She now cuts any cords of attachment you may have connected to their manifestation.

Now the stars of your wishes merge with the greater stars of the Divine's wishes, aligning your will with the Divine's and amplifying the blessings of each wish.

Tara takes you into the sphere of each star, and you merge with its light. As you become one with each Divine wish for your life, you feel, see, touch, taste, smell, and know this to be true for you right now, already and always existing in the inner realms, and awaiting miraculous manifestation in the physical realm.

The ecstasy of experiencing these holy wishes in this sphere might feel almost too much to take, but stay with it.

Star by star, you float upon and into each one, fully feeling its magic and delight.

When you have felt the total bliss of experiencing your wishes aligned with the Divine's, Tara carries you back to your ferry.

She promises you that these bright, beautiful stars will be your guiding light. And She assures you that should you ever stray, She will come to your aid to help you stay the course and realize your sacred intentions on earth as they already shine in the heavens.

She ferries you back to your lotus pond where you

can see your radiant reflection sparkling back at you. The reflection of the stars, however, has changed. There are new, bright, beautiful stars beaming back at you in blessing: your wishes ready to come true.

Tara blesses you with Her light once more, showering you with rays of starry light. And with Her blessing, you now return back to your body.

Come back to your chair, with hands in prayer pose. Thank yourself, Tara, your spirit, and the Divine for their loving support in helping you set your sights to the stars. Open your eyes and open to miracles, beloved.

POST-INITIATION SELF-CARE:

- Write down the visions you saw in each star in your journal.

- Record the feelings you felt when you experienced each wish as already true in the inner realms.

- Reflect on how often and strongly you feel these states in your present life. The gap is what keeps our wishes at bay, whereas feeling these states now is the fastest route to their magical manifestation.

- Ask Tara for guidance on how you can feel these exalted states more consistently in your life now, no matter what your outer circumstances.

- Embody these feelings more and more in your present life by following your inner Tara's loving guidance.

- Go out to see the stars at night and make your wishes upon them.

- Make wishes upon sparklers or birthday candles at each new moon.

- Take on a forty-day *sadhana* (daily spiritual practice) of chanting Tara's mantra, *"Om Tare Tuttare Ture Soha,"* 108 times each day to invite even greater blessings from Her.

Affirming Tara:

Make a wish upon a star
Set your sights heaven high.
Remember always who you are
To let your dreams take flight.

I Am Tara.

Goddess Tara

Origin: Tibetan Buddhist

Name Meaning: Swift Savioress, The one who ferries across, Star, Mother of liberation

Attributes:

- Wish granting
- Aspirations
- Liberation
- Enlightenment
- Inspiration
- Divine purpose

- Protection
- Swift aid
- Feminine power
- Tantric wisdom
- Meditation
- Manifestation

Sacred Symbols:

- Star
- Lotus
- Boat

- *Mudra* (sacred hand gestures)
- Moon
- Forest

Chakras:

- Crown
- Third eye
- Solar plexus

Elements:

- Air
- Stars

Essential Oils:

- Lotus
- Patchouli
- Sandalwood

Colors:

- White
- Green
- Black
- Red
- Blue
- Yellow

Crystals:

- Diamond
- Emerald
- Jade

Archetype in Balance:

- Inspired
- Dreams big
- Visions are aligned with spirit
- Believes in self and own dreams
- Resilient
- Spiritual
- Independent
- Wise
- Empowered
- Self-sufficient
- Purposeful
- Kind
- Solution-focused
- Clear
- Confident

Archetype out of Balance:

- Delusional/stuck in fantasy
- Doesn't believe in dreams
- Doesn't act on dreams
- Attached to outcomes
- Holds back
- Hangs happiness on future goals
- Plays small
- Uninspired
- Insecure
- Anxious
- Fearful
- Envious

Creating Balance:

- Allow yourself to dream big.

- Align your intentions and wishes with your soul through prayer and meditation.

- Visualize and affirm your dreams as already manifested.

- Ask your soul/Tara within for swift support when you need to replace fear with faith.

- Know that you are capable and worthy of manifesting your dreams.

- Stay focused and dedicated to your path.

- Do what is meaningful and purposeful to you.

- Let your work be of service to others.

- Find inspiring role models who have done what you wish to.

- Believe in yourself and your soul's visions.

- Don't worry about the how; delight in the why and what of your dreams.

- Know that you are ever guided and blessed by the heavens.

Associated Goddesses:

- Fortuna (Roman)

- Danu (Celtic)

- Artemis (Greek)

- Sarasvati (Indian)

- Rhiannon (Welsh)

- Aeracura (Celtic)

- Isis (Egyptian)

Prayer/Invocation:

Beloved Tara, as Goddess of wishes within me, help me to free myself of all limitation and doubt, and set my sights to the stars. Align my dreams with heaven's highest will for my greatest flourishing in spirit and on earth. Free me of all fear and hesitation, and help me hold true to my Divine purpose and aspirations.

Help me to graciously receive Divine guidance and support in all ways, now and always. Help me ascend to the highest heights my soul can reach, inspiring and blessing all along the way. Om Tare Tuttare Ture Soha. *So be it. So it is.*

Gateway 8

Taking Inspired Action

Initiator:
Athena, Goddess of Wisdom

Athena

> WHATEVER YOU CAN DO OR
> DREAM YOU CAN, BEGIN IT;
> BOLDNESS HAS GENIUS, POWER
> AND MAGIC IN IT.
> —GOETHE

Welcome back to earth, beloved. I hope your ascent to the heavens with Tara elevated your dreams to their most expansive potential. While She will remain the constant star lighting your way, it is our next Goddess, Athena, who will help you do *your* part in making your dreams come true.

As Greek virgin Goddess of wisdom, war, and the creative and domestic arts, Athena is the ultimate "get it done" Goddess who empowers you to take the bold, inspired action required for the manifestation of your intentions.

Athena's most popular origin story is similar to Kali's as a Warrioress who springs from another deity's forehead. The myth goes that Her father Zeus impregnated Her mother Metis, an ocean nymph known for Her crafty wisdom. After being forewarned of a prophecy that Metis's children would prove more powerful than Him and eventually overthrow Him, Zeus decided to swallow Her in an attempt to end the matter.

Soon after, He became crazed from the pangs of a headache. His blacksmith son, Hephaestus, relieved Zeus of His suffering by splitting His head with a two-sided axe, from which fully grown Athena emerged—clad with golden armor and roaring for war. Beholding Her glorious sight and ferociousness, Athena immediately became Zeus's favorite child.

Looking more closely, we see that the most powerful of the Olympian gods, Zeus Himself, gives into His fear and tries to suppress wisdom in the form of Metis by swallowing Her. But—just as Zeus is relieved when Athena erupts from His forehead—wisdom has a way of transcending fear and has the power to free us from our suffering.

And so it is with us. How often do we suppress our own inner wisdom, the voice within that beckons us to make our move and go for it? And how do we suffer when we ignore and oppress our inner callings? Thankfully, our wisdom will always find ways to get our attention. And when we finally honor it, our inner Athena charges forward, fully equipped to overcome obstacles and achieve our goals.

Now—inspired as this interpretation of Athena's origin story may be—this classical myth itself has done a profound disservice to us women. By presenting Athena as a motherless father's daughter who favors male warriors and defends Her authoritarian father's wrongdoings, Her masculine values of competing and conquering overthrew Her feminine values of collaborating and co-creating.

Athena became "one of the boys" and championed war heroes like Jason, Achilles, and Odysseus in their feats, while brutally punishing females for following their hearts. She tore a tapestry created in fair contest by the gifted weaver, Arachne, not only because it was superior to Her own, but because it exposed Zeus's philandering ways. As if this injustice weren't enough, Athena then condemned Arachne to spin forever by transforming her into a spider.

Athena even punished Her devoted priestess, golden-haired Medusa, for falling in love and sleeping with the sea god, Poseidon. As punishment for breaking her vow of celibacy, Athena transformed beautiful Medusa into a horrid gorgon. She turned her long, lustrous locks into poisonous snakes and her sweet, love-inspiring gaze into one that would turn onlookers into stone.

This veneration of Olympian Athena's loyalty to the masculine and opposition to the feminine continues to dominate what we women are taught to value and how we are expected to act if we want to succeed. There is still deep, underlying pressure for us to accomplish our goals by over-amplifying our masculine energy to be respected and valued while negating our feminine energy, resulting in a very disempowering imbalance for us. We are expected to be more man-like and suppress and sacrifice our femininity to succeed in a "man's world."

And so we push and power through, working harder and harder to the point of exhaustion, instead of honoring the wisdom of our hearts, bodies, and cycles (as this version of Athena is the intellectual virgin war Goddess whose abode is Her mind).

Whether in our professional or personal lives, harnessing patriarchal Athena keeps us in a state of endless spinning (like Arachne)—in a state of striving and never quite arriving.

When we try to invoke Athena in this guise, it becomes necessary to balance Her with other Goddesses (like Aphrodite and Tara), so that Athena's aims are connected and aligned with our hearts, bodies, and spirits, lest we turn to stone inside by acting solely from heartless strategy and only for ceaseless conquering.

There is, however, an alternative way to embrace Athena wholly in Her own right, which endows us with the ability to take wise, creative, and joyous action in the direction of our dreams.

Long before Her classic myth of emerging from Zeus's head that came about during Greece's patriarchal Golden Age (500–300 BC), "Athena was descended from the Old European (7000–3000 BC) bird and snake Goddess; She was also the community Protectress and life sustainer, and She was associated with Greek cities."[7] Her identity as a giver of crafts goes back even further to Neolithic times.

She was previously a fatherless daughter of a Goddess who independently ruled Athens and was worshiped at the Parthenon as a wise, compassionate, and maternal Goddess. She was a very accessible Goddess of the people—and *especially* of sisterhood and priestesses. In fact, Her priestesses held significant power both politically and religiously before women's roles were subjugated and eliminated in Greece's Bronze and Golden Ages.

Long before Her Olympian identity as a ruthless Goddess of war, Athena bestowed upon Her people many practical gifts of thriving civilization: spinning, weaving, metalsmithing, art, writing, musical instruments like the flute and trumpet, plows, rakes, ox yokes, horse bridles, chariots, ships, and the olive tree. She also imparted intangible gifts of knowledge, education, creativity, law, justice, mediation, self-actualization, higher consciousness, and even enlightenment.

Her worship was so pervasive that the newer Olympian religion was unable to get rid of Her. Instead, it was forced to appropriate Her into the male-dominated religion that reflected the rise in militarism and warfare. In this pantheon, She was demoted to loyal warrior daughter of a dominant male God,

7   Marija Gimbutas, *The Living Goddesses* (California: University of California Press, 2001), 158.

rather than being revered as an independent Goddess of women and men in Her own right.

In order for us women to reclaim our inner Athena for cultivating our gifts and creating our best lives, it is not Her perverted version as a defender of patriarchy that we need to resurrect, but Her true, original nature as a people's and women's Goddess that can best support us.

The older/original Athena reminds us that our work is not to endlessly fight to conquer an outer goal, because She understands that behind the longing for such a goal is really the Divine impetus to realize and actualize your true inner nature. Her role is to help you express your inner self through joyous practical action to unleash your own potential while contributing to the greater good.

Athena reminds you that you living your purpose of being your fullest, truest self is the ultimate goal. Everything else is an effect of your connection to your higher self, not the cause of you experiencing the states (happiness, peace, joy, freedom, self-actualization) of your true self.

This is precisely what eliminates the pressure of constantly putting in effort and trying, and shifts your focus to expressing, enjoying, and expanding who you are through what you are inspired to do.

> *Athena reminds you that you living your purpose of being your fullest, truest self is the ultimate goal.*

And while we do indeed need to do our part in bringing our Divine visions into form by following our inner Athena's practical wisdom, we also need to remember this key: that we are to work from the inside out, and not from the outside in.

As a Goddess who very well may have inspired Lao Tzu's wise words, "The journey of a thousand miles begins with one step," Athena will guide and support you one step at a time. She will require you to trust your Divine wisdom to show you each progressive step in the co-creation process, instead of obsessing over how and when your ultimate goal will manifest.

From this place, we co-create our dreams with ease and joy instead of trying to conquer our goals no matter the cost.

We take action from a place of inspiration, rather than desperation. We act from faith instead of fear.

We bless and release the control-freak Athena who must have a rigid plan of how She will accomplish what She wants.

We embrace Athena as our inner wisdom to give us just the next right step on our paths as we hold true to our dreams (as Tara showed us), and stay centered in our self-love (as Aphrodite awakened within us) to experience their joyful manifestation in perfect Divine timing.

Cultivating Athena's practical power is essential to taking empowered responsibility in creating our dreams. For Aphrodite alone can serve as the muse to inspire our desires without furnishing us with the focus, commitment, and discipline required to gain momentum. And Tara's bright visions on their own can keep us floating in a fantasy unless we ground Her inspired aspirations with Athena's intuitive action.

ATHENA IN ACTION

To best understand the difference in harnessing the original versus patriarchal Athena, here is how each would have you go about attracting your soulmate, if that is one of your desires:

Olympian Athena:

First of all, She would completely disapprove of your desire to have romantic love, as She punished Her priestess Medusa for this. She would instead have you focus all your energy on furthering your education or career goals, leaving no time for starting a romantic relationship.

If, by some miracle, She decided to help you with this endeavor (likely so that you can focus back on your more worthy goals in Her eyes), this Athena would have you make a rigid plan for when and how you will meet your mate.

Her plan might look like this:

1. Meet partner in next three months.

2. Move in together after six months to test long-term potential.

3. If still together, marry partner within next two years.

4. Start family one year after marriage.

She would then create a strategic plan and action steps under each milestone. For example, to check off goal number one, She may have you:

1. Make a list of what you want from your potential partner.

2. Sign up to the three most suitable dating sites.

3. Hire a matchmaker (give her a list of what you want).

4. Schedule dates with potential suitors for every Friday night for the next six weeks.

5. Check each person against the list.

6. Eliminate those who don't match 85% or more of the list requirements.

7. Go on further dates with only the long-term potentials.

8. Narrow down the top three candidates by week six.

9. Ensure the top three are marriage material, ideally meeting close to 100% of the list requirements.

10. Choose the most compatible/best suitor by end of month three.

While this type of plan may end up helping you find your partner, the approach also takes all the joy and spontaneity out of what could otherwise be a more beautiful and magical experience.

Original Athena:

Harnessing this version of Athena within you will first of all help you feel confident about your worthiness and ability to find lasting love. As Her approach is more intuitive and open, She will guide you on a gentle, step-by-step path in which love can unfold more gracefully and synchronously.

She may first guide you to become clear on what hasn't worked for you based on your past relationships. She may guide you to start journaling or hire a coach/healer to help you extract the lessons from your past relationships and heal any unconscious blocks and patterns.

Keeping only the wisdom from your past, She may

next guide you to buy a guided meditation to help you visualize the bliss of being with your beloved.

If one of your lessons from healing your past had to do with loving yourself first, She may guide you to start making small changes to demonstrate love to yourself.

As you begin to practice self-love and continue with your visualization or other tools Athena guides you to, you may find yourself feeling more whole and happy.

As you feel more vibrant, Athena may then inspire you to join a class for a hobby you've always wanted to pursue. And then, who do you end up sitting next to during your class? Your future soulmate!

This is an example of how the more balanced Athena may guide you to do your part in manifesting your dreams in a way that requires trust, patience, and the power of small, intuitive actions.

LIVING YOUR POTENTIAL

When you consciously invoke this Athena's gifts, She will also arm you with all the tools you need to bring your inspired ideas into form. She will help you strategize and get organized, but in a way that feels aligned with your values and wishes.

She will help you enjoy and appreciate each step for its own sake, instead of suspending your happiness until you reach your goal.

She will also help you to review, revise, and refine each step to help you meet your goals efficiently and successfully. True to Her nature, She will compel you to act with integrity and fairness, honoring yourself and all at each step.

Like a mother who knows and believes in her children's purpose and potential, She will lovingly push you to give and be your best.

She will not allow you to play small to let others shine.

She will inspire you to share your gifts and works publicly.

She will urge you to be the Creatress of the life you desire and deserve.

This is precisely why it was important to ask and answer the question, "Who am I?" with the Goddess Tara before awakening Athena. Because one of our greatest inner blocks is the disempowering question we all seem to ask ourselves when being called to take inspired action. The question is: *Who am I to (fill in the blank)?*

Whether it confronts us as we desire love, success, purpose, health, happiness, and all spiritual and material gifts we deserve, this fear-based question has the power to completely immobilize us even as we wish to progress on our paths.

For me, the question has shown up in countless forms, only some of which include:

"Who am I to: Meet and marry my soulmate? Have a home I love? Become a mother? Create a successful business? Live my Divine life purpose? Share my passion and work publicly?"

Meditating on the very question, "Who am I?" and coming to the blessed realization that I am Goddess manifest here to embody, experience, and express the Divine as it inspires me to has brought me the grace to move past insecurity, and compelled me to take faithful action with Athena's blessing.

And this is Her blessing to us all: to inspire action from within so we can realize our dreams without and to empower us with all the inner and outer tools we need to co-create our dreams—whether personal, spiritual, or material.

BEYOND BALANCE: CREATING HARMONY IN YOUR LIFE

Beyond supporting you on each step of your path, as the quintessential mediator, Athena will also help you create more harmony and satisfaction (going beyond mere "balance") in your life, as you seek to honor all your Sacred Feminine drives and passions.

For example, if your inner Aphrodite craves more romantic time with your partner, but your inner Kuan Yin is always busy taking care of your family, Athena will help you schedule much needed "me time" to help you to first replenish, and then guide you on how to make arrangements (reservations, babysitting, etc.) for a date night with your partner.

If you want to bring more sacredness (Wise Woman Goddess) to your workplace (Athena's domain), She may inspire you to incorporate rituals (lighting incense, praying before each task, setting intentions, creating a desk altar, playing uplifting music, etc.) to turn your office space into a sacred temple, and your work into sacred service.

Whatever your desires, Athena can help them complement rather than compete with one another.

Finally, it is important to note that as an embodiment of applied wisdom, Athena ensures we don't fall into the trap of waiting to feel motivated, courageous, or confident enough to act on our inner guidance. She knows that motivation, courage, and confidence are not required before taking action, but acquired after taking action.

It is time now, beloved, to awaken *all* of Athena's gifts to leap boldly forward into your most glorious, joyous life. You deserve nothing less. With your inner Athena awakened, you are capable in every way of creating the life you desire and deserve.

Your inner Athena knows that motivation, courage, and confidence are not required before taking action, but acquired after you take action.

PRE-INITIATION PREPARATION:

- Know the Kundalini mantra, *"Ong Namo Guru Dev Namo,"* which means, "I bow to and invoke my inner divine teacher/wisdom."

- Keep a journal and pen handy.

- Light a white candle.

ATHENA'S INITIATION: TAKING INSPIRED ACTION
Initiation Type: Guided Meditation

Sit in *sukhasana* pose (legs crossed) or half/full lotus (legs crossed and feet on opposite inner thigh/hip crease).

Begin by pressing both palms together in front of your chest. Press your thumbs into your center, the seat of your heart.

Chant *"Ong Namo Guru Dev Namo"* silently or aloud three times.

Bring your right hand up to prepare for *Nadi Shodhana* (alternate nostril breathing), which balances the yin-yang, feminine-masculine, receptive-active, creative-intellectual, intuitive-logical, and moon-sun inner spheres (including your left-right brain hemispheres).[8]

Curl your index and middle fingers down, keeping thumbs, ring, and pinkie fingers straight. Bring your hand like this in front of your nose. After exhaling all the air out, press your thumb tip onto your right nostril, blocking the air, as you inhale from your left nostril. Once you have inhaled, press the ring and pinkie down to close the left nostril and lift the thumb to exhale completely from your right nostril.

Inhale from your right, close, exhale from your left using the same finger motions as above. Repeat this for a total of nine counts on each side.

When complete, bring your breathing back to normal and gently rest your palms facing up on your knees. Use *gyan mudra* (consciousness gesture) by bringing the tips of your thumbs and index fingers together.

Staying focused on your calm, even breathing, see yourself now lifted up in a bubble of light. You are being transported into Athena's sacred temple and arrive instantly at Her celestial Parthenon in its full glory, located atop Her lush acropolis.

You find yourself at the temple doors and as they open, beautiful Athena greets you with Her priestesses.

---

8   Skip this part if you are pregnant or have respiratory issues.

She smiles and welcomes you home to the abode of your soul's wisdom.

As She guides you farther into the temple, you notice the tall white columns aligned in perfect order. There are no walls and there is no roof. There is only the crisp, blue sky above your head and cool summit air to breathe into your heart.

As you sit with Athena, She points up to the sky where you can see your wishes shining in the heavens as Tara's stars from your initiation with Her. You delight at the sight of each of your realized intentions in heaven, and Athena stands with you to help them manifest on earth.

Athena asks you to focus on the star (the dream) that is most important to you right now. As you look upon it and feel the bliss of all the possibilities it holds, Athena begins to open all of your spiritual communication channels.

She starts by placing Her hands above your heart and shining white, silver, and gold light into your heart to awaken your clairsentience (clear/intuitive feeling).

She next raises Her hands above your ears, shining these lights through them to open your clairaudience (clear hearing).

She places Her hands over your third eye (forehead), and beams the three lights into it to awaken your clairvoyance (clear seeing).

She finally hovers Her hands over your crown to awaken your claircognizance (clear knowing).

All your intuitive channels are now glowing and spiraling in perfect harmony.

You are completely receptive to feeling (heart), hearing (ears), seeing (third eye), and knowing (crown) your Divine guidance.

You now ask Athena, "What is my next Divinely-inspired and aligned step in co-creating my dream?"

Bring your awareness into your heart and notice what feels like the best next step.

Raise your awareness to your ears to hear your next step (Divine guidance sounds clear, loving, and empowering).

Bring your awareness to your third eye and see what your next step is. Notice any visions or impressions.

Bring your awareness to your crown and know what your next step is.

If you don't feel you are picking anything up, continue to breathe and trust. Stay open and unattached. Some channels may be stronger than others, and you can develop the ones you may not be receiving from with practice.

Now simultaneously feel, hear, see, and know what your Divinely-inspired next step is.

If any fears come up around this, share them with Athena. If you need more details or clarification, just ask Her.

She will meet your fears with compassionate

strength until they subside. She will keep clarifying Her guidance until you feel you trust your next step.

Ask Her what to do. Ask Her how to start. Receive Her answers, beloved.

Now ask if there is anything else you need to do or know.

Then offer yourself in service of your highest good by saying, *"I ask for infinite Divine support, guidance, and protection in helping me do what I am guided to do—doing what my spirit and the Divine would have me do—for my best and highest good. Thank you, so be it.* Sat Nam.*"*[9]

Now that you have felt, heard, seen, and known your best next action, Athena opens your throat *chakra* and hand *chakras* (located on your palms), and fills them with Her white, silver, and gold light.

She emboldens you to use your voice to say what you are Divinely guided to say and use your hands to do what you feel called to do.

She blesses you with even more gifts—spiritual and practical tools to support your efforts so that all your actions will be blessed and fruitful.

You can now ask Her for guidance on each of your other dreams and receive Her clear and loving wisdom from within yourself.

If there is anything else you wish to ask Athena, do so.

Now She seals all your *chakras* in white, silver, and

---

9   *Sat nam* is a Kundalini mantra that means, "I am truth" or "Truth is my identity."

golden light so that your Divine light may guide you on your way as Tara's starlight shines down on you too at every sacred step of your path.

Your way is light and blessed. *You* are guided and blessed.

Thanking Athena, journey back into your body now, wiggling your fingers and toes.

Press your palms together in front of your heart again and chant "*Sat Nam*" three times to bless your initiation.

Open your eyes and commit to following through on your Divine guidance by taking your next step. Know that Athena's guidance is ever accessible within the Divine temple of wisdom that resides within you.

POST-INITIATION SELF-CARE:

- Write down your next steps immediately after your meditation.

- Commit to taking your next step within the next twenty-four hours. If it feels too big, ask Athena to break it down further until you reach a more accessible step, and then do it.

- Prioritize each step based on which dream it pertains to, and of these dreams, which is most important to you right now.

- Trust and follow through on each progressive-inspired action.

- Celebrate each step you take, no matter the outcome.

AFFIRMING ATHENA:

They made me theirs
But I am yours.

I am *everyone's* eternal inner guide
I am *everyone's* Goddess.

I honor all of your desires
And join you in making them manifest.

Meet me always within
To move forward without.

I Am Athena.

Goddess Athena

Origin: Greek

Name Meaning: Mistress of Athens, Goddess of wisdom

Attributes:

- Inspired action
- Wisdom
- Creative arts
- Domestic arts
- Strategy
- Protection
- Courage
- Clarity
- Crafts
- Weaving
- Metalsmithing
- Justice
- Intellect

- Diplomacy
- Tact
- Work/career
- Business
- Commerce
- Independence
- Self-sufficiency
- Sisterhood
- Culture/civilized life
- Community
- Agriculture
- Music
- Priesthood

- Purity
- Wholeness
- Self-actualization
- Victory
- Enlightenment

Sacred Symbols:

- Birds, especially the owl and vulture
- Snake
- Quill
- Books
- Parthenon
- Olive tree
- Golden armor (helmet, sword, breastplate, shield, and spear)
- Gorgon
- Aegis
- Lightning bolt
- Spindle
- Chariot
- Ships
- Musical instruments (flute and trumpet)
- Plow
- Rake
- Ox yoke
- Horse bridle
- Scales
- Priestesses

Chakras:

- Crown
- Third eye
- Solar plexus
- Sacral

Element: Air

Essential Oils:

- Rosemary
- Peppermint
- Frankincense
- Vetiver

Colors:

- White
- Silver
- Gold
- Blue

Crystals:

- Clear quartz
- Apophyllite
- Blue lace agate
- Citrine

Archetype in Balance:

- Proactive
- Ambitious
- Courageous
- Fair
- Independent
- Hardworking
- Committed
- Objective
- Self-aware
- Intellectual
- Inspired
- Creative
- Confident
- Thoughtful
- Discerning
- Analytical

- Conscientious
- Advocate for equal rights and fair treatment for all, especially women

Archetype out of Balance:

- Has a hard time relaxing
- Can't be vulnerable
- Does not accept help
- Needs to win at all costs
- Neglects personal life
- Workaholic
- Rejects/suppresses softer side of femininity
- Manipulative
- Aggressive
- Over-thinker
- Anxious
- Always doing, never being
- Resentful for doing it all
- Competitive
- Vengeful
- Reinforces/supports patriarchal structures and agendas
- Cold
- Ruthless

Creating Balance:

- Meditate with the *gyan mudra* (gesture of consciousness) to receive inner guidance. Sit in *sukhasana* (easy pose) with legs crossed. Rest hands on knees, palms facing up. Touch the tips of thumbs and index fingers together with your other three fingers straight.

- Own your worthiness for success.

- Take time to tune into your inner wisdom when making decisions.

- Take action based on faith and inspiration rather than fear and desperation.

- Work for the greater good.

- Take time to rest, replenish, and play.

- Pursue artistic and creative hobbies.

- Ask for and accept help.

- Spend time with other women.

- Stand your ground with tact and firmness.

- Speak your truth with clarity and compassion.

- Stay physically active.

- Indulge in physical pleasures to get out of your head and into your body.

- Enjoy and nurture your personal relationships to feel loved and supported, and move from your head to your heart.

- Trust your inner voice and guidance.

- Allow yourself to share your thoughts and feelings.

- Be fair and honest.

- Act with integrity.

- Do what you love and enjoy.

- Take pride in what you do.

- Write down your inspired actions and create deadlines that feel aligned.

- Organize and manage your actions in a planner.

- Invest in and use systems, tools, applications, and structures that support you.

- Work with an inspiring mentor or coach.

- Follow through on your commitments.

- Take inspired action before you feel confident (you will gain confidence after you act!).

- Delegate tasks that you don't have to do.

- Align your mind (ideas, plans, goals), with your heart and soul (love, inspiration, joy).

Associated Goddesses:

- Minerva (Roman)

- Maat (Egyptian)

- Brigid (Celtic)

- Saraswati (Indian)

- Isis (Egyptian)

Prayer/Invocation:

Beloved Athena, as Goddess of wisdom within me, help me to align the ideas of my mind with the light of my soul and love within my heart. Help me to act with integrity, clarity, and graceful tenacity as I take inspired action towards the realization of my dreams. Help me to trust and follow my inner guidance with confidence and joy.

Guide me at every step, and keep me present and focused along my journey. Help me to appreciate exactly where I am and fully enjoy the process of reaching my goals. Help me to realize and actualize my fullest potential and express my truest self in all that I do. Help me to feel successful, whole, and worthy just as I am. Help me to surrender the outcomes of all my intentions and actions to unfold for my highest good and the highest good of all. So be it. So it is.

Gateway 9

HONORING YOUR PATH

INITIATOR:
LILITH, GODDESS OF FREEDOM

Lilith

> LIVE WHERE YOU FEAR TO LIVE.
> DESTROY YOUR REPUTATION.
> BE NOTORIOUS.
>   —JALALUDDIN RUMI

With Athena's blessing, you now know your next step, beloved. *Will you take it?* Because the gap between knowing what we must do and what we actually do can be a fearsome one to close.

That is because, like our next initiatory Goddess Lilith knows, honoring yourself can cost you your security, reputation, relationships, and more along the way.

Like Lilith, you must be willing to do what you must do and hold true to what is most sacred to you no matter the consequences—and there will be consequences. Because when you take a stand to commit to what you most value—whether it's your well-being, freedom, joy, health, success, relationships, time, energy, passion, or dream—others may get upset, angry, and disappointed. They may guilt, judge, threaten, or shun you. And, as Lilith is about to show you, you have to be able to expect and accept this if you are to live in integrity with yourself.

In Jewish mythology, Lilith precedes Eve as Adam's first wife. Unlike Eve, who was made after, from, and for Adam, Lilith was created from the same earth and at the same time as Adam. She was created as his equal.

When Adam demands Her to lie beneath him during sex, Lilith refuses to take this subordinate position, claiming that as his equal, She will not place Herself "beneath" him.

Adam persists to pressure Her into submission. Lilith finally has Her "Fuck this shit!" moment and uses Her magical powers to obtain eagle wings so She could flee Eden. She flies into the wild sea where She can be unbound and free.

Upon Her escape, Adam pleas to his fatherly God, "Sovereign of the universe! The woman you gave me has run away."[10]

Hearing his plea, his father-God sent three angels to bring Lilith back. Adam's God ordained that if Lilith complied and returned, all would be well. But if She resisted and refused, then He would permit one hundred of Her children to die every day.

The angels did as ordered. They found Lilith playing in the sea and immediately seized Her. They delivered God's ultimatum, and upon Her refusal to accept it, they threatened to kill one hundred of Her children every day.

Lilith stood Her ground and agreed to Her banishment and punishment in exchange for Her freedom and independence.

---

10   Norman Bronznick. "The Alphabet of ben Sira" in *Rabbinic Fantasies: Imaginative Narratives from Classical Hebrew Literature*. Edited by David Stern and Mark Jay Mirsky. (Philadelphia: Jewish Publication Society, 1990).

In a later Jewish tale from the Kabbalah[11], Lilith is said to play with children who are born of men who have sex with their wives in "inappropriate ways" (naked and by candlelight) at forbidden times (likely connected to certain moon days under Lilith's rule). It is advised that when parents hear their children laughing in their sleep, they must immediately stop them and pray for their protection from Lilith.

Not only is Lilith disowned and demonized, but even those who fall under Her "sinful" influence (of the Divine Feminine gifts of pleasure and joy) and experience the delights of their bodies are punished for it. Even the innocent laughter and spontaneous bliss of their children becomes a thing to cease and fear. This is just one of the countless ways the Abrahamic religions injected fear and shame into our most primal experiences of physical pleasure and joy—which are the domain of the Goddess.

Like Athena, Lilith's classic myth perverts Her original status as a more ancient and benevolent Goddess. Where once She was revered as a Mother and fertility Goddess who brought agriculture to Her people and protection to children and women (especially in childbirth), the rise of patriarchal power subjugated and demonized Her as a night-creature who seduces and castrates men, stirs sinful desires in women, causes

---

11   *Bacharach*, "Emeq haMelekh," 84b, 84c, 84d.

miscarriages and stillborns, and kills and eats children in their sleep.

Once the venerated "Mother of All," She became the feared Mother of Demons. Once the giver and guardian of life, She became its vicious taker.

From being worshiped as Goddess to outcast as a she-demon, Lilith was abandoned and punished not only by Her husband, but by Her very creator—Her Father-God. By choosing to honor Her Divine Feminine worth and value in opposition to both patriarchs, She sacrificed not only Her place in heaven, Her marriage to Adam, and Her favor with God, but even Her own children.

Those who dare to speak and act against male will must be willing to pay unfathomable consequences: judgment, abandonment, ostracism, and even—as the children born of Lilith's free sexual unions face—death. Death to what we birth and create from our unbridled pleasure and Goddess-given *shakti*.

Yet Lilith is willing to pay every price to live *Her* life on *Her* terms. She will honor Her carnal, sexual desires. She will live with lust for life. She will relish in the delights of all earthly pleasures, for She knows that every part of earth—and Herself—is sacred.

And here, thousands of years later, we find ourselves facing similar threats. In countries even

Lilith relishes in the delights of all earthly pleasures, for She knows that every part of earth—and Herself—is sacred.

today, women are burned, stoned, and shunned for rising against oppressive structures. In Africa, their genitals—their sacred *yoni* portals to bliss—are mutilated before girls even enter puberty. In Southeast Asia and Saudi Arabia, women are killed by their own brothers and fathers for losing their "honor" when they are raped. This loss of "honor" is their broken virginity that now deems them damaged goods. A woman is punished if her body temple is violated, for it is now rendered impure for her future husband, to whom it and she belong.

Even in the Modern West, where we are protected against such atrocities, there remains invisible but palpable disdain for our full and free flourishing. It brazenly confronts us in religious, political, social, and economic circles that are still led primarily by men—men committed to forwarding patriarchal agendas and maintaining their power through control and subordination.

Individually, we experience the threats now just as Lilith did then.

The threat of losing our jobs or promotions if we are unwilling to sacrifice our personal lives.

The threat of losing our child-bearing years if we commit to building our careers.

The threat of losing respect if we want to stay home and raise our families.

The threat of losing support if we dare to commit to our dreams.

The threat of losing approval if we express our truest selves.

And even the threat of losing love if we choose to fully love ourselves.

On my own journey, I have had many Lilith initiations, and they were the proudest, most liberating moments of my life:

When, at seventeen, I was beaten by my father down three flights of stairs for stopping his verbal assault on my mother, telling her very firmly, "Mom, you don't have to put up with this shit."

When, in the same year, I refused to be forced into an arranged marriage and chose my freedom over my father's approval. He called me cold, selfish, and callous for years to come.

When, at twenty, I continued to earn my father's wrath and rejection as I refused to wear a *hijab*, stop listening to music, and learn the domestic arts instead of attending university.

When, at twenty-three, after his constant threats, he kicked me out of the house for continuing to defy his will. Upon accepting his banishment, I became the "heartless whore" who abandoned my family, while my father became the victim of my "Western feminist immorality."

When I refused my mother's pleas to return, she accused me of planning to get disowned so that I could be free to "sleep around with men." She proceeded to ask me why "all the men" only came after me when I was a seven-year-old child being sexually abused under her care.

A few years later, my mother forbade me to marry Eric because he wasn't Muslim, even though I was not a practicing Muslim myself. While a Muslim man can marry a non-Muslim woman, a Muslim woman is forbidden to marry a non-Muslim man. If she does, her marriage doesn't count in the eyes of Allah (God), her marital sex is sinful, and her children are hell-bound bastards.

My mother insisted that she would rather see me heartbroken and alone for the rest of my life than married to a non-Muslim, and that I would be dead to her if I went ahead. She completely broke my heart. But Lilith came fast to mend it. She made it even stronger, and filled it with the mother's love that I had lost at that time.

Beyond my family, I faced consequences in my professional life as well—from refusing to work during my personal time, using fear to control my teams, and being underpaid. The final ultimatum I was given was to submit to a culture of harassment (that I had taken a stand against), or resign. Like Lilith, I chose the rejection and fled on my wings of self-respect, becoming free to work for myself ever since.

While all these consequences were painful at first, they were all prices I happily paid to uphold my values, honor my desires, and live authentically.

Lilith knows that it is only through setting your boundaries that you can set yourself free. Your time, love, and energy are sacred resources, and you must guard them at all costs, spending them only on what and whom you value.

This is Lilith's gift and call to you, sister:

You must *own your no*, no matter the price, so that you may say an empowered *yes!* to yourself.

You must disobey unfair demands, no matter *their* disappointment.

You must honor your path no matter the consequence.

You must not conform, no matter the temptations.

Lilith is the Wild Woman within every woman who would rather become notorious than be refrained from bathing in the sea, howling at the moon, dancing in the forest, and making love to life itself.

She knows the price both the Goddess and Her daughters pay to honor their ways, for She is not the only one to suffer condemnation by those who fear feminine power. Like Her, they defamed Her sisters too: magical Hecate became the baby-killing hag and wicked witch, and mystical Mary Magdalene was turned into the sinful whore.

Lilith knows that it is only through setting your boundaries that you can set yourself free.

And hand-in-hand with Her sisters, Lilith implores you: *Let them do their worst!*

Let them call you a heretic, for true heresy is being untrue to *yourself*.

Let them burn you as a witch, for your ignited soul will rise from the ashes.

Let them label you a whore, for desire is your gateway to bliss, creation, and life!

Let them shun you for standing by yourself, for a Wild Woman belongs to no one but herself!

Know this: there is nothing more threatening to those enslaved by their fears than someone who dares to live freely.

And live freely you must. As a bird-snake Goddess who dwells in the dark depths of your holy *yoni* and crown, Lilith compels you to harness your untapped life-force energy to do all that you wish to do without explanation or apology.

In a Sumerian myth pre-dating Her Hebrew origin, Lilith is mentioned as *ki-sikil-lil-la-ke*,[12] where She lives in Inanna's sacred *huluppu* tree (the Tree of Life) as a serpent nested in its base and an Anzu (a lion-headed, eagle-winged bird deity) raising its young at the crown.

Mystically speaking, Lilith is the coiled serpent at the base of the spine—the Kundalini *shakti*—the primal, sexual, and creative feminine force that is released through spiritual evolution and ecstatic union. As a bird tending its younglings at the crown, Lilith is the Mother

---

12   "Tablet XII" in the *Epic of Gilgamesh*, c. 600–1000 BCE.

Goddess who nurtures the potential of our spiritual liberation.

Her serpent powers of healing, wisdom, and self-realization are again perverted as She becomes the evil snake who seduces and penetrates Eve, causing Adam's second wife made as his subordinate, to bleed. Menstruating Eve is deemed by her Father-God too filthy for Adam to touch.

But Lilith was not there to trick Eve. As Goddess of sex, fertility, women's cycles, the moon, and blood mysteries, Lilith initiates naïve Eve into her own *shakti*—the liquid red power to heal her body, awaken her intuition, and create life itself. Lilith knows that our bleeding days unleash our physical, emotional, energetic, and spiritual powers. We see and feel things more purely and potently. Lilith defines PMS as the blessed time you become a *powerful, magical Sorceress.*

She wants Eve and every woman to know her worth and own her power, no matter how hard *they* try to keep you from it. She wants you to be the authority in your life without having to seek permission from anyone or anything outside of yourself to be or do what your heart calls you to.

Lilith proceeds to tempt Eve to eat the forbidden apple from the tree of knowledge of good

Lilith is the Wild Woman within every woman who would rather become notorious than be refrained from bathing in the sea, howling at the moon, dancing in the forest, and making love to life itself.

and evil so that she may discern *for herself* what is right and wrong. She wants Eve to see the false paradise in which she is a mere servant to Adam and his father's will.

In the Bible, Lilith's invitation to Eve is described under "The Serpent's Deception":

> [*The serpent said to the woman,*] *"For God knows that in the day you eat from it your eyes will be opened, and you will be like God, knowing good and evil." When the woman saw that the tree was good for food, and that it was a delight to the eyes, and that the tree was desirable to make one wise, she took from its fruit and ate; and she gave also to her husband with her, and he ate. Then the eyes of both of them were opened ... (Genesis 3:5–7* (New American Standard Bible)).

Far from being the deceptive serpent, Lilith is the wise liberator. And She is on Eve's side. *Of course* She wants her (and everyone) to "be like God," for She knows that we are the embodiment of the Divine. She wants to free Eve and every woman (and man) from the illusion of the perfect life that comes at the price of blind obedience.

She invites us to bite into the forbidden fruit of knowledge so that we may be free to think for ourselves and decide for ourselves what is right and what is wrong. She knows this comes with responsibility and consequence, and She emboldens you to take it on.

Yes, Lilith wants you to be God-like, to have Divine authority and will in your own life. She calls you to leap boldly forward as you take the inspired action you need to take to live your most p_hysically- and spiritually-free life. Those who live freely will join you. Those who don't will no longer have the power to hold you back.

With my own family, for example, my father ended up very sincerely admitting and apologizing for his earlier "fear-based mistakes" and how he had treated me. He shared how proud he was of me for defying him and obtaining my honors degree with distinction. He spent later years nearly nagging my three younger sisters to get PhDs and even became an advocate for women in Pakistan to pursue higher education and professional careers.

My mother not only attended my Scottish-Pakistani fusion wedding, but she came to adore Eric and embrace his culture and family well before the wedding.

Even as religious Muslims, both my parents have come to accept and respect my Goddess-centered spiritual and professional path.

While I never required or ever expected their approval as I chose to honor my path like Lilith, I am endlessly grateful that doing so inadvertently helped evolve them into open-minded, kind, and supportive parents.

> *There is nothing more threatening to those enslaved by their fears than someone who dares to live freely.*

Just as She has with me, beloved, Lilith is calling you to play fully with your life, to break the shackles, and defy those who seek to rule over you so that you may live freely and perhaps even inspire others along the way. Through Rumi's words, she asks:

> *"You were born with wings, why prefer to crawl through life?"*

It is time now to awaken Lilith so that you may find your own wings and set yourself free.

PRE-INITIATION PREPARATION:

- This ritual will be most potent when done on a full-moon night.

- Get naked and wear blood-red lipstick.

- If you feel safe and comfortable, let the moonlight shine through your windows.

- Light red candles and place them in safe places.

- Have your journal and pen handy.

- Play some bewitching music that makes you feel fierce and free.

- Place a ripe, juicy red apple on your altar to eat after your initiation.

- Embark on the journey as a meditative dance, or meditate on the questions and then write them in your journal.

LILITH'S INITIATION: HONORING YOUR PATH
Ritual Type: Meditative Dance, Journaling

Begin with a slow, sensual dance to awaken Lilith's passion within you. Touch yourself. Revel in the beauty of your body.

Slowly come to sit at your altar. Keep undulating your spine in snake-like waves from your *yoni* to your neck. Switch to luscious spirals with your pelvis, belly, breasts, and neck. Move or pause as you feel guided.

Closing your eyes, see Lilith fly in through your windows. She is a sight to behold with beautiful golden hair, bare breasts, eagle wings, and taloned feet.

Instinctively, She encompasses you in Her soft, strong wings, nestling you into Her motherly bosom.

"Welcome, daughter. I have waited long for our blessed reunion."

Feeling safe and loved in Her embrace, you share with Her the dream stars you wished upon with Tara and the guidance you must heed from Athena.

She is proud and smiles at you, reminding you that you can have and do all this and so much more. But She needs to ensure that you are in integrity with what you say you want in order to support you.

She asks you to keep your desires and actions in your heart and share with Her what it is that you most value. What is most important to you?

Perhaps you share Lilith's values of freedom, independence, pleasure, joy, wisdom, magic, equality, respect, creativity, discernment, authenticity, and integrity. Perhaps you have other ones. Share them all, for She values you and all that is important to you.

When you are done, Lilith holds you tight and lifts you up, higher and higher, until you can see your life from Her eagle-eye vision.

She helps you see the gaps between what you say you want to have and do, and how you are actually being and acting in your life.

She reveals to you whether your actual actions are consistent with your deepest values.

She shows you if your choices are in alignment with your soul's priorities. *What do you see?*

Where are the disconnects? Where are you out of integrity with your truth? Where are you undermining yourself? Where are you settling and compromising?

She stirs up the serpent *shakti* at the base of your spine and calls you to scream out in unison:

"FUCK THIS SHIT!"

Scream it out as many times as you need to. They renamed Lilith the "night-screecher," so screech, sister! Hiss like a snake at all the disempowering patterns that you are ready to break free of.

Get up and dance. Spread your arms like Lilith's wings and fling aside the obstacles from your path.

When all is cleared, come and sit before Lilith again.

She now asks you Her holy questions to help you take back your power and live your life on your terms:

- What is acceptable and unacceptable to you in these situations?

- What needs to change so that you can honor yourself?

- What do you need to do to create these changes?

- What do you need those involved to do?

- What will you do if they refuse to honor you?

- What could they do if you refuse to submit to them?

- What do you need to do to be ready for any consequences?

And now, Lilith poses Her final question: *Are you ready, willing, and able to stand by yourself, no matter the outcome?*
You know you are. But should you have any self-doubt, Lilith places Her powerful hands behind your back, and chanting sacred words, gives you your own beautiful wings.

She declares:

"It is time to go forth and set yourself free,
To do what you came here to do,
And be all that you were born to be."

You thank Lilith for Her love, strength, and protection. She embraces you one last time. You bow to each other in reverence, and Lilith flies away.

Come back into your body, beloved, and ground yourself through more dance and movement if you wish.

When you are ready, blow out your candles, and prepare to soar freely in your life with the primal force of your awakened *shakti* empowering your path.

POST-INITIATION SELF-CARE:

- Eat your sacred apple, inviting it to awaken the power of truth and discernment within you.

- If you didn't during the initiation, write down your answers to Lilith's questions.

- Write down what you need to say to anyone that you need to assert yourself with, focusing on:

  - How you feel about the issues that are no longer acceptable to you.

  - What you want instead.

- What you need and are willing to do.

- What you need from those involved.

- What you will need to do for yourself if they decide not to work with you (which they are free to do).

- Follow through on what you say you will do—both to yourself and others.

AFFIRMING LILITH:

Daughters of the earth!
Shamed for all that is holy and glorious in you
Shunned for all that is the Goddess in you,
Come to me now, my children,
And let your Mother give you wings to fly!
Talons to hold your ground
And mark what is rightfully yours!
A Serpent tongue to lick and taste and suck the nectar
from your Earth Mother's sweet, full breasts!
Never again to be banished from paradise,
Ever dwelling in heaven within your own sacred nature.

I Am Lilith.

Goddess Lilith

Origin: Mesopotamian

Name Meaning: Goddess of the South Wind, Beautiful maiden, Mother of All, Female-Night Creature (Hebrew)

Attributes:

- Freedom
- Independence
- Equality
- "Hand of Inanna" (sacred sexuality)
- Desires
- Laughter
- Pleasure
- Joy
- Sexual freedom
- Creativity

- Fertility
- Childbirth
- Women's liberation
- Magic
- Moon wisdom
- Menstrual/blood mysteries
- Integrity
- Authenticity
- Defiance

Sacred Symbols:

- Bird (Anzu, eagle, owl)
- Serpent
- Lion
- Apple
- Wild sea
- Wings
- Caves
- Menstrual blood
- Tree of life
- Talon feet
- Bare breasts
- Smile
- Golden hair

Chakras:

- Crown
- Solar plexus
- Sacral
- Root

Elements:

- Air
- Water

Essential Oils:

- Red Rose
- Patchouli
- Ylang-ylang

Colors:

- Gold
- Red
- Green
- Black

Crystals:

- Garnet
- Jasper
- Obsidian
- Carnelian
- Bloodstone
- Moonstone

Archetype in Balance:

- Clear on personal values
- Honors personal values
- Remains true to self
- Authentic
- Lives with integrity
- Honors oneself
- Does what feels right
- Enjoys one's sexuality
- Makes one's own choices
- Does not require others' approval
- Values personal freedom
- Fights for fair and equal treatment
- Discerning
- In touch with one's feminine power
- Tapped into Sacred Feminine wisdom
- Commands respect from others

- Is willing to compromise only when it comes from love and dedication, not guilt and obligation

- Unafraid of authority

- Takes a stand against tyranny and injustice

Archetype out of Balance:

- Does not assert boundaries

- Compromises self to appease others from a place of guilt and obligation

- Afraid to take a stand for oneself

- Defensive

- Aggressive

- Gives one's power away

- Submits to others' will

- Inauthentic

- Doesn't honor personal values

- Vengeful

Creating Balance:

- Get very clear on your own values.

- Assess how you give your power away and take measures to reclaim it.

- Build your self-worth and value from within.

- Know yourself as an equally beloved child of the Divine.

- Speak your truth.

- Stand up for what you believe in.

- Be true to yourself.

- Be authentic.

- Own all of yourself unapologetically.

- Own your desires.

- Relish in your body.

- Honor your sexuality as sacred.

- Claim pleasure as your birthright.

- Seek only your own approval and validation.

- Trust in your own resourcefulness.

- Enjoy sensual and earthly delights.

- Be more present in your body.

- Touch the earth.

- Meditate under a tree.

- Swim in the sea.

- Dance wildly in nature.

- Go on adventures, trips, or retreats on your own to reconnect with your wild and true nature.

Associated Goddesses:

- Mary Magdalene (Christian)

- Valkyrie (Norse)

- Tlazolteotl (Toltec)

- Hathor (Egyptian)

- Freya (Norse)

- Kali (Indian)

- Venus (Roman)

- Hecate (Greek)

Prayer/Invocation:

Beloved Lilith, as Goddess of freedom within me, help me get crystal clear on my deepest values, and grant me the courage to honor them at all costs. Help me know myself as an infinitely worthy, valuable, and beloved child of the Divine and Goddess embodied.

Help me to respect myself and command respect from others. Help me to have the courage to walk away from people and situations that are not in integrity with who I am and what I deserve. Help me to seek only my own approval and let this be enough.

Help me to be true to myself and express my most authentic nature with delight and without apology. Help me to speak my truth and stand my ground, come what may, for I have wings to fly!

Help me to honor my Divine Feminine gifts in all their glory and elevate the treatment and position of women on this earth. May I live freely, passionately, and fully like you. So be it. So it is.

Gateway 10

Harnessing Your Triple Goddess Cycles

Initiator:
Yemanya, Goddess of the Womb

Yemanya

ON HER FIRST BLEED,
A WOMAN MEETS HER POWER.
DURING HER BLEEDING YEARS,
SHE PRACTICES HER POWER.
AND AT MENOPAUSE,
SHE BECOMES HER POWER.
—NATIVE AMERICAN SAYING

Having received your wings from Lilith, I hope you are feeling completely wild and free, beloved. While Lilith has empowered you to honor yourself, as Goddess of the moon and women's sexuality, She knows that you must deepen into the mystery and magic of your *womb*manhood to fully flourish on your path. And so, with Her blessing, She entrusts you now to Her sister, the African Goddess Yemanya, to initiate you back into the wisdom of your womb.

As you learned with Aphrodite, our *yonis*, wombs, and sacral *chakras* are our portals to Divine passion, pleasure, and bliss. But as your next initiatory Goddess, Yemanya will show you, your womb is also the center of your Divine Feminine power to continuously conceive, create, and transform.

As women, we carry an untapped reserve of magical energy in our wombs and learning how to harness it is essential to our individual and collective empowerment. Yemanya shows us that whether or not we are menstruating, reconnecting with our bodies' sacred cycles as well as the phases of the moon is the pathway to unlocking our dormant *shakti*—our vital feminine life force—for this is the source of Her life-giving powers.

Yemanya is a Yoruba Orisha, one of the seven natural forces of the Gods of the African pantheon. As Goddess of the ocean and moon, She birthed Divine and earthly creations through Her ocean womb. She is the loving Mother of All (including the most powerful Orishas), who heals and nourishes us with Her maternal waters. Without Yemanya—without water and the womb—life would cease to be.

Her worship is so ancient and Her nature so beloved, that during the African diaspora, She was embraced by the New World and syncretized with Mother Mary (as star of the sea) and other female saints (as Our Lady of Seafaring and Our Lady of the Conception) in the Americas. Beach festivals are still held in Her honor on New Year's and holy days in Brazil, Uruguay, and Cuba.

Yemanya is the depths of feminine intuition. She is the cyclical nature of women. She is the phases of the moon and menstrual cycle. She is the embodiment of the ancient sacred feminine trinity of *Maiden-Mother-Crone*:

As Maiden, She is the playful surface-level

Yemanya is all the phases of the moon and menstrual cycle. She is the embodiment of the ancient Sacred Feminine trinity of Maiden-Mother-Crone.

waves of the ocean, mermaid Goddess of fertility, festivity, sensuality, friendship, beauty, desire, pleasure, joy, ideas, and inspiration.

As Mother, She is the life-giving waters, pregnant Goddess of love, conception, childbirth, parenting, family, community, growing, nourishing, abundance, opportunities, celebration, creativity, and birthing our desires into being through inner power rather than overt force.

As Crone, She is the dark depths and violent waves of the ocean, bare-breasted Goddess of death/transformation, feminine wrath, ancient wisdom, women's mysteries, healing, prophecy, protection, mysticism, magic, the unconscious, and dreams.

When we lived more naturally in agrarian times, we were in sync with the rhythms of the ocean, moon, and our bodies. In Goddess-centric and indigenous cultures, we even honored and celebrated our initiation into womanhood at menarche with sacred ceremonies.

We would gather in women's-only spaces in tents and moon lodges when we bled as the girls and wise women tended to us. We rested. We retreated. We replenished. We offered our red-hot blood back to Mother Earth to nourish her sacred soil and honor our intimate connection with her. We delved into trance and meditation to receive Divine messages and prophecies and shared this wisdom with our tribes.

We would emerge from each cycle more powerful

and radiant, ready to start a fresh cycle with more clarity, vitality, and vibrancy.

Since our departure from living in oneness with Mother Nature, we have lost our connection to the cycles of the earth and moon, and, as a result, to the mysteries of our own wombs. We came to emphasize and value the solar cycle over the lunar, which favors doing over being and action over receptivity.

In losing our connection to the moon, we have disconnected from the inner, spiritual cycle of conception, creation, and transformation we experience through our menstrual cycles (menopausal women and women without physical wombs still experience this energetically).

The result is that we keep pushing and never pausing to fully honor and cultivate our womb wisdom. We effort and strive, aiming to get results from more work and doing. We struggle to live in an ever-conquering vertical, masculine path rather than harnessing the birth-life-transformation cycle of our feminine nature. We forget that, like Yemanya, we can create flourishing, harmonious lives for ourselves by flowing with our innate rhythms rather than struggling against them.

This is what Yemanya is now here to support you with, beloved. As *Mama Wata* (Mother of the Waters), She is all of our womanly waters: the slippery wetness of arousal, the explosive nectar of orgasm, the fertile fluid at ovulation, the blood shed at menstruation, the water breaking in labor, and the tears of rage and grief during your moon-time. As the essence of water, She is the very element of your womb, intuition, and feelings.

As ocean and moon Goddess, She is the ebb and flow of your inner nature and the cyclical nature of all of creation. Her multiple powers manifest in us during our initiations as Maiden, Mother, and Crone, and during every phase of our menstrual cycle:

Maiden Goddess
Initiation: Menarche
Moon phase: Crescent and waxing
Menstrual phase: Follicular/pre-ovulation

Mother Goddess
Initiation: Childbearing years
Moon phase: Full
Menstrual Phase: Ovulation

Crone Goddess
Initiation: Menopause
Moon phase: Waning and dark
Menstrual phase: Premenstrual and menstruation

This sacred feminine trinity, which we experience within us every month and at our Maiden-Mother-Crone life initiations, mirrors the Divine dance of birth, life, and death through all of creation. Like the ebb and flow of the sea, the phases of the moon, the change of seasons, and the dance of the universe itself, we *womb*men are blessed with a mystical and primal connection with all cycles of life.

We are called to trust in uncertainty as we conceive and gestate new life—whether a baby or idea—in the dark, unseen waters of our wombs. We are supported physically and spiritually in nourishing what we are growing with patience and care. We are held in the threshold of the unknown as we labor and birth our conceptions into being. We are comforted and empowered as we release what needs to die and transform.

Embracing our womb wisdom helps us live from our Divine, Goddess-given power and flow with the waves of life. This is why being out of sync with our sacred cycles can be so painful and often leads to a multitude of hormonal imbalances and health issues.

On my own journey, the wounds of sexual abuse and shame around my body and sexuality had deeply traumatized my womb. In my teens, I dreaded getting my period, as it meant being bedridden with pain for days, for which I took Mefenamic acid (a prescription-strength pain reliever).

> *We **womb**men are blessed with a mystical and primal connection with all cycles of life.*

My periods were also very heavy and I bled for seven to eight days. I would often feel light-headed and sometimes even faint. All this amplified by the hypersensitivity, rage, and frustration I felt caused me to resent being a woman and curse that "time of month." I was already experiencing depression, anxiety, and post-traumatic stress disorder from years of abuse, and the monthly onset of my period only intensified all the other symptoms.

My doctor advised I go on a birth control pill, but my Muslim family was against this as they didn't want to encourage sexual activity. In university, when I was able to see a doctor on my own, I went on the pill for the next few years. All my symptoms did subside, and frankly, I was grateful for the relief. In fact, I thought the pill was a gift from God as it freed me of what I deemed to be my womanly miseries.

As I have shared, however, I was initiated into another dark night of the soul by the grace of the Goddess in my mid-twenties. In the depth of the depression, I knew I needed to face this wave with a Sacred Feminine approach. Like we did with the earlier initiatory Goddesses, I delved into the pain and allowed myself to process it with their Divine love and support. In the process of healing my sexual traumas, the Goddesses guided me to re-learn the feminine mysteries and sacredness of my body temple.

Since I was able to heal the depression naturally, I felt called to come off the birth control pill as well. I didn't want to do anything drastic, so I began to apply the feminine wisdom that I had learned about my menstrual cycle first.

While still on the pill, I gave myself a few months to support the needs and harness the gifts of each phase of my cycle. Doing so brought such healing, magic, and joy to every part of my life that I was able to transition off the pill with ease.

Since being pill-free and continuing to honor my cycles, I no longer experience the intense symptoms I did in my teens, as I was blessed to heal the deeper, underlying psychological, spiritual, and even karmic issues behind the symptoms. I do, however, get mild cramping, low energy, and am extra sensitive during my moon-time.

The difference is that now I look forward to and embrace everything that arises during this special time, because I understand that each "symptom" is actually a gift. It is a sacred invitation from my inner Crone Goddess to deepen into Her wisdom—an invitation I am honored to accept each month.

In fact, I have a special moon-time Goddess kit to nourish myself during this sacred time, and I invite you to create your own. Mine includes: soothing and detoxifying herbal teas, essential oils, massage bars/oils, herbal compresses, a hot water bottle, aromatic bath bombs, dark chocolate, red and black pajamas, red bedsheets, a journal, a smudging wand, and a special musical playlist. I even wear red clothes and nightgowns to honor my bleeding days.

Having a dedicated moon-time Goddess kit for when you menstruate (or during the final waning/dark moon days if you don't) is a radical act of self-love and a powerful path to healing as a woman. I invite you to create such a kit for yourself, my sister, and watch your relationship with your period completely transform.

To harness the full magic of our cycles, let us now receive the Sacred Feminine wisdom of Yemanya's womb for yours, beloved. While this Triple Goddess guidance is based on the monthly cycle of the moon, don't worry if your cycle is shorter or longer, doesn't sync with the moon phases, or if you no longer menstruate. You can work with the rhythms of your own cycle or follow the phases of the moon. Honor your own womb and inner moon wisdom. In time, you will find your own flow and welcome each phase with grace and joy.

HONORING THE MAIDEN GODDESS: INTENDING, INITIATING, ENJOYING
New and waxing moon, follicular phase, (generally lasts seven to ten days)

This is a time of feeling physically, mentally, and emotionally clear. You'll be the most focused and energized. You are most connected to the intellectual energy of your third eye and life force energy of your root and third eye *chakras*. Harness this phase by:

- Setting new intentions for the month ahead.

- Getting inspired as your creative juices are flowing.

- Planning, strategizing, and initiating personal and professional projects.

- Scheduling your most intensive physical or mental tasks.

- Trying or learning something new.

- Socializing with friends and colleagues.

- Playing and having fun!

- Staying physically active with more rigorous workouts like Pilates, martial arts, power yoga, running, high-intensity interval training, and circuit and strength training.

HONORING THE MOTHER GODDESS: CREATING, CELEBRATING, CONNECTING
Full moon, mid-cycle ovulation phase (three to four days)

This is a time of feeling the love. You are sending out irresistible pheromones and relishing in all things sweet, sensual, and expansive. You are most centered in the graceful expression of your throat *chakra*, love in your heart *chakra*, and desire in your sacral *chakra*. Harness this phase by:

- Making love with yourself or your lover.

- Cooking and sharing cozy meals with loved ones.

- Creating and advancing personal and professional projects.

- Expressing your love with words, touch, and other thoughtful gestures.

- Having heart-to-heart conversations (especially based on your reflective time during the menstrual/Crone phase).

- Presenting, speaking, teaching, and leading.

- Celebrating all that has come into fruition.

- Enjoying sensual pleasures, beautification, and self-care.

- Working with and supporting others and allowing yourself to be supported in turn.

- Going on dates and enjoying romantic experiences.

- Staying physically active with more sensual movement like dance and yoga.

HONORING THE CRONE GODDESS: REVIEWING, RETREATING, RELEASING
Waning and dark moon: Luteal (ten to fourteen days) and menstrual phase (three to seven days)

As you enter the premenstrual and menstrual phase, your physical, emotional, and mental energy draws inward. The hypersensitivity is actually your increased psychic awareness. You feel things more intensely on every level and become acutely aware of situations that don't honor you. Harness this powerful phase by:

- Reviewing and re-examining what is and isn't working for you.

- Setting and asserting your boundaries.

- Re-organizing or decluttering your space.

- Completing, revising, and re-evaluating personal and professional projects.

- Delving into your rage, pain, and frustration through journaling or therapy.

- Doing inner healing work.

- Going inward through meditation, or meditating for longer periods.

- Recording and interpreting your dreams.

- Practicing divination through Tarot or oracle cards.

- Spending time in nature.

- Performing releasing ceremonies through smudging, forgiveness, or cord cutting.

- Shielding your potent psychic energy by covering yourself with your clothing, crystals (red jasper, black obsidian) or through energetic shielding (visualize yourself in a protective bubble of light).

- Taking time to rest and replenish (get more sleep, take naps).

- Minimizing highly social engagements around your period, especially with people who trigger you.

- Keeping yourself warm and cozy with hot baths and hot water bottles.

- During menstruation, detoxifying with herbal teas, vegetable juices, saunas, steam rooms, dry brushing, and massages.

- Using a menstrual cup to preserve and offer your blood to Mother Earth by pouring it into her soil (or pour it into your plants).

- Staying physically active in gentler ways, like restorative yoga, walks in nature, and even taking the first day or two off.

Isn't it interesting, beloved, that the phase we tend to neglect or resent the most—the menstruation phase—offers us the most ways to harness our power? The Crone is given the least amount of respect and reverence in our culture, and it is precisely because She bears the sacred gifts of discernment, intuition, independence, healing, transformation, and truth. She is the Wild and Wise Woman you become when you are crowned into your Crone-hood.

As you explore the suggestions for harnessing your cycles or syncing with the moon's cycle, I know from the depths of my own womb, that you will unleash the beautiful, powerful gifts of your own. Your womb is the vessel of pleasure, creation, wisdom, and transformation. It is a living oracle you can tune into at any time to make choices aligned with your highest good.

Now simply allow Yemanya to lovingly initiate you deeper into your womb wisdom, so that you may flow with the sacred rhythms of your Triple Goddess cycles.

PRE-INITIATION PREPARATION:

- Create an altar for Yemanya with seashells, sand, ocean or spring water, pearls, moonstone, and/or turquoise.

- Light white or blue candles.

- Keep your breasts bare and wear a white or sea-blue flowy skirt.

- If you have them, wear silver, seashell, pearl, moonstone, or turquoise jewelry.

- Play ocean-wave music as well as the *Yemanya Assessu* chant/song if you can easily find it.

YEMANYA'S INITIATION: HARNESSING YOUR TRIPLE GODDESS CYCLES
Ritual Type: Guided Meditation and Movement

Sit comfortably in easy meditation pose (legs crossed). Play your ocean music, and begin to sync your breath with the sounds of the waves. Inhale through your nose and send the breath down into your womb, gently squeezing your *yoni* in and up (avoid if menstruating or pregnant). With each exhale, release and relax your *yoni*, feeling it open all the way through its lips as you breathe out through your mouth.

Slowly start undulating your spine, thrusting your pelvis forward and back, letting the movement ripple up and down. Breathe in as you round your back, breathe out as you send your tailbone back and chest forward. Pause if you wish, and restart whenever you feel guided.

With eyes closed, visualize yourself sitting on an ocean shore. It is night, and there is little light as the moon is dark. Slowly, Yemanya emerges from the depths of the ocean, and floats over to you on a wave.

Bare-breasted, She is adorned in moonstone, sea-shell, pearl, and turquoise jewels, and She wears a deep-blue seven-layered skirt that grazes the soft sand beneath Her feet.

She smiles and embraces you in a loving, maternal embrace. She holds your hand and takes you closer to the ocean where the waves play at your feet.

With the next wave, She conjures forth the memory of your first period. She shows you what happened when your *yoni* first bled. She asks:

- How did you feel (physically and emotionally)?

- Who did you tell?

- How did they react?

- Who was there to welcome and guide you?

- Were you celebrated or shamed for entering *womb*manhood?

- What did you think of your blood?

- What were the messages you continued to receive about your period and becoming a woman?

- How did you continue to experience your period?

Allow yourself to recall and feel all the sensations and emotions of your periods. As you do, Yemanya now transports you back to your first period, so you see yourself young and bleeding.

As the red-hot blood flows down your legs, this time, it is welcomed and honored. Yemanya rejoices at the sight of your blood, and Her mermaid maidens join you in celebration.

Yemanya wipes the blood from your legs, and draws spirals with it on your womb and forehead, initiating you into your womb wisdom. She keeps Her hands on your womb and third eye, blessing you with sacred chants and prayers as Her mermaids chant back in delight.

They adorn you in beautiful white flowers and magical jewels. They bring you a chalice of red wine. Yemanya pours a drop of your holy blood and Her own in the glass and invites you to take a sip. Notice any repulsion you may feel, and know that this is just fear of your own power.

Slowly, you sip this holy wine and ingest its potent magic. The holy wine now awakens and unleashes all the feminine mysteries that lay dormant in your womb from your first bleed through all periods until now. The mysteries will continue to unfold and are yours to understand and own.

As you invite waves upon waves of women's wisdom to flow through you, Yemanya and Her mermaids invite you into the ocean, where you float in a bubble of silver and blue light, and Yemanya transforms into Her mermaid form.

Your blood merges with the ocean. As you release your holy blood, Yemanya welcomes it into Her womb, where She is nourished by its rich potent minerals. She offers you Her cleansing, healing ocean waters in turn. With each wave of love, She purifies and heals you of all shame, fear, guilt, and grief trapped within your womb.

As you are cleansed, She now takes you deep into the depths of Her ocean, where you meet your own Crone Goddess nature. She is your inner Wise Woman, Healer, and Warrioress. She has a message for you about what is no longer serving you. She too places her hands on your third eye and womb, and reveals to you the truth about a situation you have been avoiding.

She shows you how this issue no longer serves you.

She shows you all the elements that are out of integrity. She tells you whether this needs to be released or healed, and offers her wisdom to help you understand your next steps. Perhaps she speaks in metaphors and symbols, or through feelings and sensations. Trust whatever comes, for this is her secret language.

Allow yourself to feel the fullness of her raw emotions as they are your unfiltered truth. When you're done, she bids you goodbye and gives you her blessing, knowing fully that you are wise and powerful like her, for you *are* her.

When you rise up upon the waves with Yemanya and Her maidens, you see a beautiful crescent moon shining its light upon you and the vast ocean.

Yemanya is ready to initiate you into your Maiden Goddess gifts, and so She transforms your legs into a mermaid tail of your own. Now you, too, are playing with the maiden mermaids and you are joined by sweet dolphins. You swim, dance, sing, and rejoice. You feel so vibrant and clear and energized.

You look upon the waxing new moon and feel a surge of inspiration and desire flow from your womb center and out through your third eye. As it flows out of your third eye, it meets with the moonbeams and bursts into sparkles. They spiral towards the moon, and as the moon continues to wax, the moonbeams return to you with ever-increasing light. Each time the light flows back to you, you get more energy, clarity, and inspiration. You do what you feel called and guided to do while still playing in the ocean with great pleasure and joy.

Yemanya guides you to swim back to the shore where you emerge with Her wearing a seven-layered blue skirt of your own. When you look at the ocean, you see the moon is full and glorious, illuminating everything around you. All the life in the ocean is glistening and dancing.

You feel yourself glowing from the center of your belly through your heart, and Yemanya draws a full moon over both. You feel the milky white light from your *yoni* and heart shine so brightly, that it extends to all life around you. It uplifts everything and everyone nearby.

Your heart overflows with gratitude for the radiant blessings you already have in abundance in your life. You begin to dance a spiral dance with Yemanya, feeling orgasmic waves of rapture and pleasure overtake you. You feel your desires growing into fullness inside you, and as you spiral in ecstasy, they flow through from your *yoni* into beautiful manifestation.

You see and celebrate all that you have birthed and tend to it like a loving mother. You share the bounty of your heart and gifts with Yemanya and your loved ones, and all dance in celebration.

As you bring your hands to your womb and heart, Yemanya begins to draw the symbols of the Triple

Goddess—the new crescent, full, and waxing crescent moons—on your womb, heart, and third eye.

She welcomes you into the full nature of your Maiden-Mother-Crone power, and asks that you honor their presence within you through each phase of the moon and your own womb's cycles.

You know you will, for it is your birthright as a *womb*man to own and hone all the gifts of your sacred cycles.

Yemanya gives you one last message to embrace your moon wisdom. And then, upon a moonbeam-lit ocean wave, you gently flow back into your body to the here and now.

Continue to breathe into and out of your *yoni*, beloved. When you are ready, place your hands on your womb, and with a smile radiating from its ocean depths, slowly open your eyes.

With your hands still on your womb, close your initiation by chanting Yemanya's sacred song, which celebrates Her as the ocean Mother of All Life:

Yemanya Assessu
Assessu Yemanya
Yemanya Olodo
Olodo Yemanya

POST-INITIATION SELF-CARE:

- Write down the messages or insights you received in your meditation with Yemanya and your inner Maiden, Mother, and Crone Goddesses.

- Bathe in a natural body of water, or create a mermaid bath with sea salt, white flowers, and a drop of blue food color or a blue bath bomb.

- Drink a lot of water to continue to clear and heal your womb.

- Keep dancing (to Yemanya or festive African or Brazilian music) throughout the day to integrate the energy of your initiation.

- Wear your crystals and jewels throughout the day.

- Place a moonstone crystal beside your bed to increase your feminine intuition.

AFFIRMING YEMANYA:

I am the waves of the ocean
And all faces of the moon.

I am the treasure chest of wisdom
Hidden deep within your womb.

I am the Maiden, Mother, and the Crone
I am here to bring my daughters home.

I Am Yemanya.

Goddess Yemanya

Origin: African (Yoruba)

Also Called: Yemaya, Yemoja, Yemoya, Yemanja, Yemonja, Mama Wata, La Sirene

Name Meaning: Mother whose children are the fish, Mother of waters, Mother of all

Attributes:

- Womb wisdom
- Creation
- Feminine mysteries
- Intuition
- Cycles
- Moon phases
- Triple Goddess (Maiden-Mother-Crone)
- Natural cycles
- Birth-life-transformation
- Menstrual cycle
- Fertility
- Conception
- Pregnancy
- Birthing new beginnings
- Menopause
- Granting wishes

- Dance
- Play
- Joy
- Abundance
- Sensuality
- Manifestation
- Protection

- Love
- Friendship
- Community
- Family
- Dreams/the unconscious
- Maternal love
- Mother healing

Sacred Symbols:

- Ocean
- Seashells
- Mother of pearl
- Moon
- Fish

- Mermaids
- Sea creatures
- Waves
- White flowers
- Long, blue, seven-layered skirt

Chakra: Sacral

Element: Water

Essential Oils:

- Ylang-ylang
- Patchouli

- Jasmine

Colors:

- Blue
- White
- Silver

Crystals:

- Moonstone
- Turquoise

Archetype in Balance:

- Creative
- Fertile (physically and/or creatively)
- Harnesses the gifts of one's feminine cycles
- Honors one's Maiden-Mother-Crone powers
- Takes time for self-care
- Lives in oneness with the moon/lunar cycles
- Knows when to do something and when to be
- Lives a healthy lifestyle
- Listens to one's feminine intuition
- Deeply connected to one's body
- Loves and honors one's womb, body, and sexuality
- Flexible
- Flowing
- Births desires into being with ease and joy
- Manifests from the inside out

Archetype out of Balance:

- Stagnant

- Fatigued

- Creatively blocked

- Works excessively hard

- Health and hormonal issues

- Cannot birth desires into being

- Disconnected from moon and natural cycles

- Menstrual challenges and imbalances

- Feels overwhelmed by feelings/sensitivity

- Unable to access intuition

- Suppresses unhealed and raw emotions

Creating Balance:

- Embrace all phases of your feminine cycles.

- Hone the gifts of each phase of your menstrual cycle (follow Maiden-Mother -Crone suggestions).

- Plan activities by the lunar cycle.

- Work with a holistic nutritionist/naturopath to eat the best diet, take supplements, and herbs to best suit your health and hormonal needs.

- Chart your cycle to plan your month around your energy levels.

- Create the feminine way: conceive the idea within your womb-heart, nurture with inspired joyful action, labor with strength and grace, birth in its own timing, celebrate what you create with loved ones and community.

- Schedule time to rest when you will be menstruating or during the waning/new moon.

- Celebrate your feminine initiations with sacred ceremony (menstruation, pregnancy, menopause).

- Swim in the ocean or take sea salt baths to heal your sacral *chakra* and womb.

- Spend time under the moon through all its phases.

- Clear your womb energy by smudging your lower abdomen.

- Nourish and strengthen your *yoni* through Mayan womb massage and steams, *yoni* egg practices, and pelvic floor exercises (avoid if pregnant).

- Meditate and place hands on your womb to receive its messages and wisdom.

- Attend or host new and full moon women's circles.

Associated Goddesses:

- Ixchel (Mayan)

- Arianhood (Welsh)

- Hina (Polynesian)

- Hathor (Egyptian)

- Luna (Roman)

- Hecate (Greek)

Prayer/Invocation:

Beloved Yemanya, as Goddess of womb wisdom within me, help me to harness all the magic of my Sacred Feminine cycles, and the cycles of Mother Moon. Help me to honor my inner Maiden, Mother, and Crone equally, and receive their gifts fully.

Help me to nourish my body and my womb with sacred self-care. Help me to be in sync with my natural cycles of inspiration, creation, and transformation. Help me to uncover the mysteries of my sacred blood and activate its power fully in my life.

Let me celebrate the rhythms of my body and the bodies of all women. Help me create sacred sisterhood and resurrect the times of our ceremonial red tent gatherings, so that we may together reclaim our Divine womb wisdom to heal and bless ourselves and our world. So be it. So it is.

Gateway 11

RECEIVING YOUR BOUNTY

INITIATOR:
PACHAMAMA, GODDESS OF
ABUNDANCE

Pachamama

HAIL TO OUR MOTHER,
WHO POURED FORTH FLOWERS IN
ABUNDANCE,
WHO SCATTERED THE SEEDS OF
THE MAGUEY (AGAVE),
AS SHE CAME FORTH FROM
PARADISE.

—AZTEC HYMN

I hope you are feeling deeply connected to your body and womb wisdom with Yemanya's initiation, beloved. As She has illuminated the mysteries of the moon and your womb, Yemanya has reminded you that, like Her, you hold the power to birth, nurture, and transform whatever it is you desire in perfect, Divine timing.

When you begin to sync the wisdom of the previous initiatory Goddesses with Yemanya's Triple Goddess guidance, you will begin to find great ease, flow, and joy in your life as you co-create your dreams into being.

The next initiatory step on your path then, is to prepare to *receive* your blessings with the help of Andean Goddess, Pachamama.

Pachamama's name means "Mother Earth" and that's exactly what She is. She is the maternal provider, nourisher, and sustainer of our physical life. The mountains are Her breasts. The caves are Her womb. The waters are Her blood. The winds are Her breath. The song of birds and crickets and cicadas are Her voice. The rhythms of day and night are Her heartbeat. The change of seasons is Her menstrual cycle. The flowers, fields, vegetation, insects, and animals are Her beloved children. *We* are Her children.

And while She provides for all Her children equally and in abundance, many of us struggle deeply and constantly with receiving Her boons. As women, especially, there are some very specific ways that we block our good:

Receptivity Block #1: Undervaluing Your Worth and Over-giving to Others

Like Pachamama, we women are great at giving of ourselves to others. We may tirelessly take care of others' needs before tending to our own:

We may do more than our share around the house and not bother asking our partners or children to do their part.

We may compensate for our colleague's lack of commitment by doing their share of the work.

We may always give our friends a shoulder to cry on, but never burden them with our own struggles.

We may be the first person to offer help and the last one to ask for it.

When we do this without filling our own cups first and replenishing them after, we can end up feeling depleted and run dry, like a barren desert instead of a lush oasis.

We may be the ones who always understand, accommodate, and support, but never express our own needs (and secretly hope that others will intuitively know or ask). When we get into such a pattern in any relationship (and every situation is a relationship), then, like Pachamama, our generosity can be devalued and taken advantage of.

Instead of appreciating us, those whom we keep giving to can end up expecting more and more *from* us, while losing more respect *for* us. The more we feel them withholding their acknowledgment, the more we may seek to earn or force it. We expect that our thoughtfulness and care will be noticed and reciprocated without realizing that if we give to those who don't value us, we will create damaging and codependent patterns that do no good to either party.

If we continue to over-give, our actions—no matter how outwardly noble—become contaminated with the energy of bitterness and manipulation. Instead of feeling like abundant providers, we turn into resentful martyrs. We seek to indebt others into paying us back with whatever deeper inner need lies at the root of all our giving. It becomes a toxic game of control rather than a joyous flow of mutually enjoyed blessings.

Holding such toxic energy within ends up repelling rather than attracting the abundant love, prosperity, opportunities, and support we desire. In order to free ourselves of these self-sabotaging patterns, we must understand what the deeper cause of our over-giving (not to be confused with honoring our responsibilities and genuine generosity) stems from: beneath the compulsion to over-give is the wound of undervaluing our own worth.

Based on our earlier life experiences and conditioning, we may feel that we alone are not enough. Because we don't feel inherently enough, we resolve to compensate for this inner lack by outer over-giving. We can over-give with our time, energy, love, money, resources, support, and even our own bodies.

Those of us who are highly sensitive or natural caregivers are especially prone to over-giving. While it may come from a sincere intention to help, love, or heal others, in doing so, we not only deprive ourselves of the mutual love and support we deserve, but we also deprive those we are trying to rescue from learning their own life lessons and growing on their paths.

We expend our disguised ego energy outwards, instead of drawing on our Divine, infinite *shakti* (feminine life force energy) to support ourselves and empower—not enable—others.

> *Beneath the compulsion to over-give is the wound of undervaluing our own worth.*

How to Stop Over-Giving:

1. Reclaim Your Sacred Self-Worth

In order to invite in the abundant blessings we desire, we must create more harmony in our giving and receiving or the natural flow gets blocked. We begin this process by not blaming others and focusing instead on healing ourselves. Specifically, we must gently and tenderly heal the feelings of undeservedness that perpetuate the pattern of over-giving. This can be done very thoroughly with the shadow and forgiveness work we delved into earlier with Goddesses Inanna-Ereshkigal and Kuan Yin.

2. Create Healthy Boundaries

The second step is to summon Pachamama's rightful wrath in drawing boundaries and commanding respect from those who exploit us. The Andeans believe that when Pachamama gets angry at Her people for dishonoring Her, She creates earthquakes as a dragon who shakes beneath the mountains. The locals heed Her warning by immediately making offerings and sacrifices to Her to atone for their mistakes and re-earn Her good graces.

Like all Goddesses, Mother Earth is multifaceted.

While Her dominant nature is one of a loving, creative, and nurturing Mother, She takes no issue in summoning Her rage when it's called for. This is what She teaches us, too: that no matter how compelled we feel to always give, we must also be willing to take a stand for our worth and value.

It is our sacred right to honor the gifts we share, and it is our responsibility to ensure that others do too. Even if it means letting out a little rumble now and again to make those who exploit you shudder. This is where Pele, Kali, and Lilith can also support you in asserting your boundaries, beloved.

3. Fill Your Cup First

The third step in healing our wound of unworthiness and symptom of over-giving is by giving to ourselves first and often. The deeper essence of the Mother Earth Goddess archetype is the ability and necessity to nourish and support ourselves. This is challenging for us women to do because we can feel guilty for spending or "splurging" on ourselves. We might even feel that getting our share would take away from another.

This is when we must remember that Pachamama is the embodiment of abundance, not lack. She is the physical manifestation of infinite creativity

It is our sacred right to honor the gifts we share, and it is our responsibility to ensure that others do too.

and ever unfolding expansion. And so are you. And so is every person.

There is an infinite source of supply and sustenance already within you (and everyone), because it is who and what you truly are. *You are abundance.* Denying yourself good is denying your own Divine nature and Goddess-given inheritance.

In this way, you can re-frame whatever you spend on yourself not as an expense but as an investment. And above any tangible benefit, your own well-being and happiness is the priceless return you deserve to receive when you invest in yourself.

Another way to alleviate any guilt in caring for yourself is by remembering that the more you allow yourself to receive, the more you can give from a place of fullness to those who warrant your generosity.

4. *Trust the Wisdom of Your Body*

The final step in healing the habit of over-giving is by giving only when it is in integrity with your values and priorities. A simple and effective way of assessing whether or not you are giving from a place of genuine generosity (instead of a lack of worthiness) is by tuning into your body:

See yourself doing what you are considering,

> *There is an infinite source of supply and sustenance already within you, because it is who and what you truly are. You are abundance.*

and then notice if your body feels light and expansive, or tight and contracted. It is that simple. If giving feels good and comes from a place of fullness and joy, give with joy. If it is coming from a place of insecurity, the need to control, fear of consequence, or inner lack, it will not feel good and your body will tell you. Honor this. Honor yourself. Honor the other.

Receptivity Block #2: Believing in Scarcity Instead of Abundance

Our next greatest block to receiving the abundance that is our Divine birthright is by focusing on lack rather than abundance. Even if we consciously desire prosperity, we may harbor deep unconscious beliefs and fears around material good—and money in particular—that inhibit its manifestation in our lives, no matter how hard we work to acquire it.

While Mother Earth and the entire universe are lavishly abundant, if we harbor a scarcity consciousness, we never feel like we have enough. This feeling leads to us believing that we need to compete with others for limited resources, because we don't believe there is enough for us all.

While competition has been a pillar of the patriarchal approach to wealth and success, the Sacred Feminine approach invites us to collaborate instead.

Pachamama teaches us that there is plenty, and that every sentient being has a role to play in creating harmonious living on earth.

There is no competition, because each of us has our own unique contribution to make, and each one of us has the same Divine right to be abundantly supported as we do. As we each play our parts with the faith that there is more than enough for us all, we see that supportive community—and sacred sisterhood for us women—helps us flourish both individually and collectively.

Another consequence of a scarcity consciousness is that when we compete and compare, we can't possibly be content with what we have as there will always be those who have more. We end up feeling envious instead of blessed and stifle our supply of good by dismissing what we already have.

But it can be challenging to shift to an abundance consciousness when we receive mixed messages. On the one hand, our society places a high value on being wealthy. On the other, deep-seated religious values around money still contaminate our Western ideals of success and prosperity.

Here is just one example of the pursuit of money being condemned in the Bible:

"No one can serve two masters. Either you will hate the one and love the other, or you will be devoted to the one and despise the other. You cannot serve both God and Money." (Matthew 6:24 (New International Version)).

When religion makes money the root of all evil, those of us who are spiritually inclined feel that it is greedy, selfish, or sinful to be prosperous. We may even feel like it is more spiritual or noble to shun material wealth completely.

But as physical safety and stability are root *chakra* concerns (the first energy center at the base of your spine), when you don't feel financially secure, you can't cultivate the higher *chakra* gifts of creativity, joy, service, and self-actualization. Any "starving artist" or ascetic healer will tell you that worrying about their basic needs is far from conducive to their ability to work joyfully and effectively.

Ironically, the world's religious organizations are themselves profoundly wealthy. One only needs to look at their monuments to see that massive amounts of money are required to construct their institutions. The ordained leaders are either paid salaries or have their material needs completely met so that they can live lives of service. Their ability to be charitable also depends on their ability to amass funding. And yet, even while they require money to thrive, they often condemn their followers from desiring and acquiring it.

Since Mother Earth as a Goddess represents living abundantly in Her physical paradise now, (rather than waiting to live in the spiritual paradise in the afterlife), condemning money is yet another way of minimizing and shaming all that is earthly and feminine.

But Pachamama is here to remind you that it is rightful and holy for you to be wealthy, beloved, because the Divine itself *is* infinite creativity, expansion, and abundance.

There is no shame in claiming your Divine inheritance, and there is no glory in denying yourself the Divine's loving support in all ways—material and spiritual.

CREATING AN ABUNDANCE CONSCIOUSNESS:

1. Look to Pachamama

A simple and powerful practice to transform a scarcity consciousness is to notice all the abundance already around you. Can you count the blades of grass in a garden? The leaves on a tree? The drops of water in a river? The grains of sand on an ocean shore?

No matter how lack-focused our minds may be, we need only look to Mother Earth to realize that nature is abundant, and that abundance is natural.

No matter how lack-focused our minds may be, we need only look to Mother Earth to realize that nature is abundant, and that abundance is natural.

Whenever you find

yourself feeling that there isn't enough, simply go out in nature and consciously acknowledge the abundance that surrounds you. Marvel at how you are connected to this abundance and know that you are as much a part of it as it is a part of you.

2. Give Thanks for the Abundance You Already Have

The quickest route to shifting out of jealousy, envy, and self-pity is by giving thanks for the blessings already present in your life. No matter what your circumstances, give thanks for every form of abundance you already have:

- Give thanks for the money you do have.

- Give thanks to your job, employer, office, clients, business, and colleagues.

- Give thanks for the roof over your head.

- Give thanks for a bed to sleep on.

- Give thanks for a safe place to live.

- Give thanks for every morsel of food.

- Give thanks for the clothes on your body.

- Give thanks for clean water.

- Give thanks to your mode of transportation.

- Give thanks for electricity.

- Give thanks to all the services available to you.

- Give thanks for your health (health *is* wealth).

- Give thanks for all the people in your life: those you love and those who teach you to grow.

Give thanks even to the relationships where money triggers you:

- Give thanks to your billers for the services they provided.

- Give thanks to your lenders for believing in your ability to pay them back (with interest, no less).

When you create the habit of deliberately appreciating what you already have, you begin to live in a state of contentment rather than comparison. You realize that, in truth, you could never stop counting the blessings already abundant in your blessed life.

3. Celebrate Others' Prosperity

When we envy others' good, we are affirming our own belief in scarcity. But when we view others' success as evidence that anything is possible for us all—that if they can have it, so can we—we are affirming our belief in abundance.

Celebrating others' good centers us in the truth that we are all one. In realizing that we are one, we remember that we are all equally worthy children of the Divine. And so, when one of us is happy, healthy, and wealthy, we are all uplifted by this grace.

If you find envy creeping up, your task is to compassionately do the inner shadow work to heal the wound of unworthiness that makes you feel that you can't have what others do.

You can then transform your envy into inspiration, and focus on what part of their good it is that you, too, desire. You can reclaim your right to desire this by giving way to your inner Aphrodite, Tara, or Yemanya. You can then summon your inner Athena to take inspired action to co-create this desire in the way that best aligns with you.

Celebrating the good that is bestowed upon others opens us to receiving our own, because we are joyously honoring the abundance available to us all.

4. Share Your Bounty

The final step to shifting outside of scarcity and into abundance is by practicing generosity. Whether we give our prayers, love, time, or money, sharing our own good demonstrates our faith in abundance.

Although charity is condoned by all religions, the patriarchal path remains one of constantly acquiring more and more. The feminine path is one of circulation as this is evident with Mother Earth's own nature.

When we share our good, we are coming from an inner state of having plenty now and trusting that we will continue to have plenty. Just as Pachamama knows that She is able to replenish Herself by drawing on and creating from Her inner source of *shakti*, we know that we can afford to give because we have and will get more from the infinite well of abundance within us.

In fact, one of the quickest ways to receive what we want is to give it. This is because giving is a testament to ourselves and the universe that "I have more than enough, so much so that I can afford to give it." This state of inner abundance attracts all forms of outer abundance to us.

But in order to give freely and joyfully, we must be tapped into this inner source of abundance, which is precisely where our final greatest block to receiving arises...

RECEPTIVITY BLOCK #3: FOCUSING ON THE OUTER SUPPLY

When we wish to become more abundant, we often think in terms of attracting more money. We place our focus and faith towards the outer supply. This is one of the greatest illusions that disconnects us from the actual source of supply, which is the *Divine within*.

Pachamama's fruits and flowers are the outer manifestations of what is unseen: the roots connected to the heart of Her *shakti*—the soul of Pachamama. Mother Earth creates Her bounty from Her inner *shakti*, Her inherent life force. The bounty in itself is the effect of the deeper cause, which is Her true creative power. This same source of *shakti* is also within you.

Like Pachamama, you are the essence of abundance. Your good does not come from anything outside of yourself. It comes from your connection to the infinite source of abundance *inside* of yourself.

When you awaken to this truth, you no longer block your good by assuming that your supply must come from your job, business, clients, partner, investments, and so forth. These are all the means through which your connection to your own *shakti* channels abundance. They are not the cause. The money or supply you receive through any channel is the direct effect of your connection to the inner source of supply.

Applying this to Pachamama, money is the fruit on the tree, and your faith in and connection to the Divine is

> *Your good does not come from anything outside of yourself. It comes from your connection to the infinite source of abundance inside of yourself.*

the roots of the tree—the invisible true cause of the bounty that flourishes on the surface.

CONNECTING TO THE INNER SOURCE OF SUPPLY:

1. Shift Where You Place Your Faith

The first step in connecting with the inner source of your supply is by simply shifting your focus from the outer effects of material good (money) to its inner cause. Affirm to yourself that the source of your supply is *within* you.

Take back the power you gave away to other channels (your employer, clients, family, investments) and place your full trust in Pachamama and the Divine within to always abundantly meet and exceed all your needs and desires.

2. Feel Abundant from the Inside Out

The next natural step in connecting with the inner source of supply is to feel abundant on the inside in order to manifest it on the outside.

This is where the earlier gratitude practice can prove very helpful in embodying the feeling of plenty. When you feel rich within, you attract riches without.

3. Be Open to Receiving through Many Channels

Don't limit yourself to how your abundance should come to you (a promotion, new job, contract, bonus, etc.). Allow and open yourself to receive your good in miraculous, joyful, and unexpected ways.

You don't have to struggle to earn your good through limited ways. Like Pachamama, simply express the inner *shakti* within you as you feel called and inspired to, and let good flourish from and to you. *It will.*

Through Her own beautiful example, Pachamama reminds you that just like one of Her countless fruit-bearing trees, your connection to your inner *shakti* within is the roots. Your inspired action is the watering and tending. Your faith is the sunshine. And the bounty of fruits you harvest is the beautiful end result of all of this.

It is time now, beloved, to merge with Pachamama, and allow yourself to receive your good by reconnecting with the powerful *shakti* rooted within you both.

PRE-INITIATION PREPARATION:

- If you're doing this indoors: place on your altar a cornucopia of fruits, a bouquet of flowers, money, and/or anything that represents abundance to you.

- Light red, green, or gold candles.

- Wear any gold, precious stone, or other jewelry you have.

- Play rainforest music with nature sounds in the background.

- If you can, be in nature: find a serene spot to sit, ideally under a lush and vibrant tree.

PACHAMAMA'S INITIATION: RECEIVING YOUR BOUNTY
Ritual Type: Guided Meditation

Whether you are indoors or out, come and sit in easy meditation pose (legs crossed). Rest your hands on your knees and face your palms up.

Close your eyes and begin to focus on your breath. Inhaling through your nose, breathe deeply into the base of your spine or perineum (root *chakra*), and exhale out through your nose.

As you begin to relax, envision beautiful roots growing from the base of your spine into the ground. See them spiral down, deeper and deeper, through all the layers of Pachamama, until you reach Her heart center.

Here, you can feel Her red and golden *shakti* throbbing from Her core. As you reach your roots into Her center, She takes them in, and anchors you into Her heart of abundant, maternal love.

Her infinite flow of *shakti* begins to rise through your roots, spiraling upwards until She enters the base of your spine. You can see the state of your root *chakra* as She begins to flow through it. You hold all your deeply-lodged beliefs (from your upbringing, culture, religion, family lineage, and even past lives) around your safety, security, sustenance, and stability here. Notice the form that all your scarcity-based beliefs take in your root *chakra*.

Whatever shape, size, or form you sense these to be in, breathe into them deeply and affirm, *"I give these old beliefs that (fill in the blanks) to Pachamama for cleansing and transmutation so that I may be free to flourish in all ways."*

Allow Pachamama's powerful and loving life force to swirl through your root *chakra*, and trust in Her wisdom to direct Her energy where and how you most need it. All you need to do is receive. Affirm, *"I allow myself to receive full Divine support and supply."*

As Her *shakti* purifies and frees your root *chakra* of all blocks to you receiving your good, see your root *chakra* pulsate with red and golden light. She replaces the energy of all your old, scarcity-based beliefs with your true, abundant essence.

With your root *chakra* radiant and ignited, She spirals Her *shakti* up through your ascending *chakras*. Each *chakra* receives the nourishing support and strength from your root, from your own Divine *shakti*. Pachamama continues to send Her own *shakti* through you too.

Supported and ignited by this Divine power, all your *chakras* begin to spiral in perfect harmony as you allow yourself to receive their bountiful gifts:

- Your glowing orange sacral *chakra* opens to receive pleasure, joy, and creative inspiration.

- Your bright yellow solar plexus centers you in your Divine worth and value.

- Your lotus pink and green heart accepts and expects the balanced flow of giving and receiving.

- Your sapphire blue throat empowers you to assert your needs and boundaries with firm grace.

- Your clear indigo third eye holds the vision for your most abundant and fulfilling life.

- Your violet, thousand-petaled crown invites the heavens to fill you with peace, expansion, and contentment.

With all your *chakras* empowered by your inner *shakti*, you see yourself as a sacred tree. Your golden red roots are anchored into the heart of Mother Earth, your body becomes the thick, strong trunk of this sacred tree.

Your arms extend out to become branches. As *shakti* flows through you, countless green leaves and colorful flowers and fruits start growing from your branches.

Pachamama's *shakti* begins to spread all around you, creating many more lush, fruit-bearing trees everywhere. She continues to create lavish vegetation, fields of golden grains, and flowing rivers and waterfalls surrounding you in Her heavenly sanctuary on earth.

Magical fairies flutter about, tending to these abundant gifts. Pachamama emerges from the earth before you, adorned in a red and gold gown and covered with precious jewels.

She smiles at you lovingly, and opens Her arms out. "Enjoy this all, my child," She says, as She welcomes you to eat Her fruits, smell the flowers, play in the water—just receive Her bounty.

You notice that as you partake in each gift with love and deep reverence, your appreciation causes even more life to grow around you. Each fruit you eat with gratitude and a sense of worth is replenished manifold.

As you see your garden of abundance spread far and wide, you think of your beloved tribe: your family, your friends, your community. You invite them to partake in this abundance of supply, which sprouts forth from your own inner *shakti*.

If you see anyone taking advantage of your generosity, Pachamama—as Her dragon self—shakes beneath the mountain and rumbles just enough to make them tremble a little. As She does, you speak your truth to them about how you expect to be treated in exchange for sharing your good. See them awakened to your truth and power. They either commit to valuing you or simply leave.

Now as you look around, only those who honor you and Pachamama remain in your circle. You all rejoice. With open hearts, they begin to share their own gifts with you. They make offerings to Pachamama as well, honoring Her as the Earthly Mother.

You and Pachamama receive all their love with your own wide, open hearts. All this beautifully balanced giving and receiving flows and circulates to you all in ever-expanding abundance.

You send the infinite abundance out to everyone you know and keep radiating it out until it reaches everyone on earth. You see our entire human and animal family having our needs completely met, feeling and being safe, secure, and supported.

Mother Earth is aglow, peaceful, and happy that all Her children are provided for in all ways, and living in harmony with Her and one another. Your heart wells up with bliss and gratitude, and you send this love down through your roots into Pachamama's own heart. She receives it graciously, and sends you back even more. You send Her back even more.

You both continue this exchange, noticing how it circulates into ceaseless flourishing within and all around you.

Relishing in this infinite exchange, you begin to come back into your body. Still feeling rooted and anchored in Pachamama, you come fully back and open to receive your bounty as it flows from your inner source of *shakti*.

POST-INITIATION AFTER CARE:

- Continue to be in nature, and immerse yourself in Pachamama's abundant beauty.

- Make a hearty stew or soup for yourself of red foods (red kidney beans, tomatoes, red onion) or root vegetables, and enjoy it yourself and/or share with your loved ones.

- Write down all the blessings you are already grateful for.

Affirming Pachamama:

The bounty of my breast is yours
The love of my heart is yours
The safety of my embrace is yours
The power of my *shakti* is yours

Every earthly good is yours
All of my abundance is yours.

I Am Pachamama.

Goddess Pachamama

Origin: Indigenous Andean, Inca

Also Called: Mama Pacha, La Pachamama, Mother Earth, Good Mother

Name Meaning: Mother Earth

Attributes:

- Abundance
- Nature
- Fertility
- Receptivity
- Cycles
- Material good
- Physical pleasures
- Stability
- Security
- Support
- Shelter

- Sustenance
- Safety
- Maternal love
- Generosity
- Community
- Circulation
- Harvest
- Gratitude
- Boundary setting
- Sacred rage

Sacred Symbols:

- Dragons
- Corn
- Lamas
- Cocoa leaves
- Mountains
- Seeds
- Incense
- Smudging plants
- Trees
- Plants
- Flowers
- Fruits
- Vegetables
- Animals
- Insects

Chakras: Root

Element: Earth

Essential Oils:

- Sandalwood
- Cedarwood
- Cypress
- Angelica

Colors:

- Red
- Green
- Brown
- Gold

Crystals:

- Garnet
- Ruby
- Bloodstone
- Red agate
- Red jasper
- Red aventurine
- Red tiger's eye

Archetype in Balance:

- Abundant
- Secure
- Stable
- Supported
- Has an inner sense of safety
- Grounded
- Grateful
- Generous
- Financially savvy and responsible
- Creative
- Content
- Celebrates others' success
- Strong sense of community
- Receptive
- Gives and receives in balance
- Has healthy boundaries

Archetype out of Balance:

- Struggles financially
- Insecure
- Unstable
- Isn't or doesn't feel supported

- Feels anxious and unsafe

- Ungrounded

- Ungrateful

- Stingy

- Hoarder

- Stagnant

- Competitive

- Jealous

- Discontent

- Has trouble receiving

- Over-gives

- Undervalues self

- Can't draw boundaries

Creating Balance:

- Uncover and release negative beliefs around money and wealth.

- Create and affirm positive and empowering beliefs about money and wealth.

- Forgive your family, community, and self for instilling negative beliefs about money.

- Find inspiring role models of people who are wealthy, healthy, happy, and generous.

- Count your blessings before going to bed, or whenever you feel insecure.

- Transform envy into inspiration.

- Celebrate others' success as evidence of what is possible.

- Ask for and accept help and support.

- Say no when you need to.

- Spend time in nature and notice all the

abundance around you.

- Ground into Mother Earth by visualizing your roots connecting into Her.

- Walk barefoot on the grass.

- Pay your bills on time and with gratitude.

- Send blessings to all current channels of your abundance (job, employer, business).

- Set aside money for yourself (savings, dreams, future goals) every time you get paid.

- Donate to charities you believe in (Pachamama loves those that support the environment and animals).

- Gather with friends, family, and community members through potlucks.

- Market your passions and accept money for doing what you love.

- Treat Mother Earth with respect and reverence (buy earth-friendly products, recycle, compost organics, plant trees, volunteer at an animal or environmental organization).

- Keep a basket overflowing with fruits and vegetables on your dining or kitchen table.

Associated Goddesses:

- Gaia (Greek)

- Mawu (African)

- Changing Woman (Native American)

- Lakshmi (Indian)

- Abundantia (Roman)

- Demeter (Greek)

- Ceres (Roman)

- Damara (Celtic)

- Fortuna (Roman)

Prayer/Invocation:

Beloved Pachamama, as Goddess of abundance within me, thank you for clearing my roots of all past experiences of lack. I release the hold of old beliefs and ask that all their effects be cleared.

Anchor my roots into your heart center so that I may receive the infinite flow of your Divine shakti and love. I open myself to receiving all my good, and claim my inheritance of spiritual and material riches that come to me with ease, flow, and joy.

Thank you for ensuring that I always feel and am secure, safe, and abundantly supported in my earthly life. Thank you for awakening my connection to the eternal source of all good and prosperity already within me as it is within you. I accept these gifts fully and with deepest gratitude. I ask that all beings everywhere be safe, secure, and supported.

May we all live in reverence and harmony with you. May we respect all life and honor all your bountiful gifts. May we lovingly support your flourishing as you support ours. So be it. So it is.

Gateway 12

RECLAIMING YOUR INNER WISE WOMAN

INITIATOR:
BRIGID, GODDESS OF ALCHEMY

Brigid

EVERY WOMAN WHO HEALS
HERSELF HELPS HEAL ALL THE
WOMEN WHO CAME BEFORE HER
AND ALL THOSE WHO WILL COME
AFTER HER.
—DR. CHRISTIANE NORTHRUP

As a woman, you are a born alchemist. You are a magical Sorceress. You are a powerful Healer. You are a prophetic Oracle. You are a High Priestess. You are a miracle worker. *You are a Wise Woman.*

All these abilities are already yours, for they have always been within you. Opening yourself to harnessing these Goddess-given gifts is best supported when you feel and are deeply grounded and nourished. Now that Pachamama has seen to this, are you ready to let your next initiatory Goddess, fiery Triple Goddess Brigid, ignite your magical powers, beloved?

Brigid is the Celtic Goddess of healing, magic, creativity, divination, and blacksmithing, born with a flame shining from Her head. She is the Divine spark within the center of your own being that has the power to turn lead into gold—intentions into manifestations, ideas into creation, illness into health, and darkness into light.

Brigid is the Divine spark within the center of your own being that has the power to turn lead into gold.

As we are approaching the end of your journey, Brigid is here to help alchemize all the work you have already done and awaken the spiritual gifts you are now ready to wield. She is here to burn away anything else that no longer serves you and transmute anything that could hold you back from living in your full, feminine power.

Brigid as Your Inner Alchemist

While Brigid is indeed a patron of blacksmiths, the deeper meaning of this aspect of the Goddess is as the ultimate alchemist. Alchemy is an ancient process of transformation through which base matter such as lead is turned into more valuable matter, such as gold. Spiritually speaking, the lead is the unconscious darkness that can impede our path to the golden light of wholeness and illumination.

Unlike spiritual teachings that encourage eliminating the ego, inner alchemy is the process by which the flame of your consciousness illuminates and transmutes the unconscious parts of yourself.

As Triple Goddess, Brigid offers us both the three aspects and three stages of alchemy:

The three essential aspects of alchemy are: a substance to be transformed, a container to transform in, and a means to transform the substance. In inner alchemy, the substance is the parts of your unhealed self. The container is the sacred space and surrender you offer to the process. The means is the flame of your Divine spark.

In the first stage of alchemy, there is the *blackening*. This is the deeply painful process of facing the hidden, dark, and volatile parts of yourself. It requires having the courage to fully feel all of your wounds. It requires a surrendered witnessing of the dissolution of your old self and false attachments (the lead) as they burn in the fire of your conscious awareness. This is what you did with Inanna-Ereshkigal, Pele, and Kali.

You continued your work with these Goddesses in the next stage of inner alchemy, known as the *whitening*. Here, you can see things from a higher perspective (with Sige) and are willing to release what no longer serves you.

This stage requires further cleansing and puri-fication of toxic substances (self-sabotaging and disempowering patterns) that emerge through the burning. It requires healing your wounds with compas-sion (as you did with Inanna and Ereshkigal). It requires bravely facing and obliterating your fears (as you did with Kali). It requires freeing yourself with forgiveness (as you did with Kuan Yin). Once achieved, you attain a state of healing, wholeness, and clarity—all gifts from Brigid as much as the previous Goddesses.

The third and final stage is the *reddening* (sometimes

Syma Kharal

this is the fourth stage, with *yellowing* being the third). This is where you transcend the past and transform into the golden Goddess Aphrodite, filled and overflowing with Divine love and completely present to your life. You are illuminated with the eternal flame of your spirit from the inside out.

You attain Tara's (your own spirit's) wisdom and create new goals that are aligned with your soul's highest aspirations.

You apply your wisdom in action through Athena. You honor your path with Lilith's strength.

You flow with your life as Yemanya.

You flourish through your activated *shakti* from Pachamama.

And you reclaim your inherent connection to the Source of all through Brigid, becoming a clear channel of miracles for yourself and others.

Can you see, beloved, that you already have gone through the process of alchemy, and are ready to assimilate its magic more fully now?

As you come to integrate this process, Brigid gifts to you Her tools for alchemy: the substance of your dark matter, the cauldron (container) of surrender, and the fire of your soul's ever burning flame.

She asks that at any time you find yourself

> *When you reclaim your inherent connection to the Source of all through Brigid, you become a clear channel of miracles for yourself and others.*

getting triggered, that you be willing to place the lead of your unhealed wounds into Her fire. She gives you Her cauldron by inviting you to create a sacred space by lighting a candle at your altar and dedicating time for meditation, reflection, and prayer.

She will fuel the fire of your spirit—no matter how dim it may seem to you at times—so that you may courageously burn, transmute, and transcend all you need with your inner Brigid's strength of a Warrioress. She will connect you to the Source of all healing and miracles. She will illuminate your path, so that you may walk in grace and presence upon your soul's journey on earth while blessing and uplifting all with your inner light.

You, too, are born with Brigid's eternal flame. Fully embrace that you are a natural alchemist and Wise Woman, and use the fire of your soul's spark to constantly transmute whatever dark matters surface on your journey. In doing so, you not only grow in your own spiritual power, but you inspire women (and men) to ignite their own.

You don't have to try to actively heal or guide others to accomplish this. Because whether or not you intend to, you will empower those around you to reclaim their inner alchemists when they see the shining example and path that you are blazing forward. When you awaken Brigid's fire within you and constantly tend to Her flame as Her priestesses did for centuries, you naturally light the way for fellow sisters to live in their own Wise Woman power.

And we need this, sister. Because while we are all equally Divine, we are also uniquely designed. Your own light, wisdom, and healing gifts are so needed so we can see what is possible for us too. We need and are waiting for the light and magic that is yours alone to shine.

Brigid as Your Inner Healer

When we are able to hold the space to heal ourselves through the process of inner alchemy, we become potent vessels of miracles for ourselves and others. As a beloved miracle worker, Brigid healed Her people of all kinds of diseases and could even breathe life back into the dead. Her healing powers came from an alchemical mix of Her many additional powers.

Beyond fire, Brigid's sacred symbols are also wells and milk. Just as fire is the element of transmutation, water is the element of cleansing and regeneration. And milk is the nourishing liquid of life.

When we tend the inner flame and let its light transmute our inner darkness, we ignite our own healing gifts.

When we replenish our inner wells (our mind-body-soul) through sacred self-care, we water the seeds of vitality and new life.

When you awaken Brigid's fire within you, you naturally light the way for fellow sisters to live in their own Wise Woman power.

When we tenderly

nourish our hearts through the milk of self-love, we invite the power of Divine love to work miracles through us.

Brigid being born with the burning flame on Her head is the same Divine spark of Goddess-God within *you*. When you accept and treat yourself as a sacred extension of the Divine, you become a potent and powerful vessel for its love and light to flow through you.

This is by no means to suggest that you try to be pure and perfect. Rather, it is about taking loving and empowered responsibility for your own healing and holding space for others as they open up to theirs—without trying to take on their inner work for them.

You don't actually have to do anything to heal others. Simply being centered in your own Divine spark and letting its flame shine in its full glory will uplift and bless everyone around you.

If, however, you feel called to delve more deeply into the healing arts, you can count on your inner Brigid to be the ideal ally. She is the medicine and Wise Woman already inside of you who will guide you to the healing modalities that will best harness your Wise Woman gifts.

Whether it is through herbs, crystals, divination, counseling, midwifery, earth magic, alternative or medical healing, yoga,

> *When you accept and treat yourself as a sacred extension of the Divine, you become a potent and powerful vessel for its love and light to flow through you.*

astrology, or any other healing art, Brigid will give you the Divine clarity to pursue the practices that most align with your passions and path.

You will know you have found the Divine right fit with a practice when learning about it feels more like remembrance rather than new information. This is because, as a woman awakened to her spiritual self, you have very likely already lived many lives as a Healer, Priestess, and Wise Woman. When you learn the time-less wisdom of the ancient spiritual teachings, you awaken dormant knowledge seeped deep within your own marrow—in the memories locked in your cellular DNA. The truth of these teachings resonates immediately and activates your latent, but readily accessible, inner gifts.

Because these gifts can feel so natural for you, you may not even realize you have them until you step back to consider how others pick up on them. If you have found that people always turn to you for guidance, that friends and even strangers start telling you their problems without you having to ask, then this is a sign that your healing gifts are already awakened, my fellow Priestess.

My husband Eric was so in awe when he started to observe something that I was just used to: complete strangers begin to tell me their life stories and trials, completely unsolicited by me. Sometimes they can barely even speak English, but they feel so compelled to share their pains with me that they manage to find the words as I hold space for them.

If you similarly find that others naturally turn to you for counsel, and that you intuitively know how to support them, whether it is through your words of wisdom, healing touch, or loving presence, please take this as a sign that you are a gifted Priestess, beloved.

You are a light-worker. Especially if you yourself have healed through personal traumas and awakened your spiritual gifts, in doing so, you very likely chose to turn your *karma* (spiritual lessons) into your *dharma* (spiritual purpose) in this lifetime. Heed the call, sister, for those who will be inspired by your journey and blessed by your gifts are waiting for you.

If you desire to express your healing gifts through the creative arts of writing, teaching, speaking, painting, dancing, designing, singing, or any other form of art, Brigid again is your Goddess.

She will give you the Divine inspiration to concoct magical creations. She will give you the courage of a Warrioress to put yourself out there and offer your gifts publicly if you wish. She will set you ablaze and empower you to shine as brightly as the summer sun. As midwife, She will support you fully

When you learn the timeless wisdom of the ancient spiritual teachings, you awaken dormant knowledge seeped deep within your own marrow—in the memories locked in your cellular DNA.

in persevering, no matter the labor pains, until you birth your desires into being.

The only thing you need to do is trust and follow Her guidance, and honor your sacred calling as a vessel for healing and miracles. Remember, though, that no matter what your gift or practice, you yourself are not responsible for healing others. As the Sorceress, you are connecting to the Divine Source, and offering yourself as its humble but powerful conduit.

Your only responsibility is keeping yourself centered in your own spirit and in your intention to be a clear channel of love, peace, and blessings. Even if you conduct healing work on others, your role is simply and only to offer your gifts with sincerity, clarity, and integrity. See yourself as the Goddess's vessel, see your recipient as already healed, whole, and blessed, and let the rest go as you surrender the outcome to be for their best and highest good.

Whether or not you feel called to pursue a path in the healing or creative arts, know that you are a channel of miracles, regardless. You heal simply and always through your own light. So keep it burning fiery bright.

The role of the medicine woman is innate and natural for you. You require neither the permission nor a platform to be a Wise Woman, because *you already are one*. By embracing your own spiritual gifts, you reclaim your Sacred Feminine power and carry forward the ways of the Wise Women, honoring those who came before you, and inspiring those who will come after you. In claiming your own spiritual powers, you heal the lineage of women through all of time.

HEALING THE WITCH WOUND

If reading about being a Wise Woman is at once inspiring and terrifying, you likely hold the collective wound of condemnation and punishment of feminine wisdom, my sister. And I hold you so tenderly here, because I know only too well the fear that can arise when we simultaneously feel called to hone and share our spiritual gifts, and yet fear ambiguous and dire consequence. This fear is not as unfounded as you may think given the history of what has been inflicted upon us Wise Women in centuries past.

While the Church syncretized Goddess Brigid as a Saint in the Middle Ages, by the time the Christian Inquisitions began in twelfth-century Europe, pagan healers and Wise Women were no longer safe to practice their crafts. As the "witch craze" intensified over the next few centuries, more and more women were convicted of witchcraft and tortured and executed by the masses.

The witch-hunts reached their peak during the late-sixteenth and mid-seventeenth centuries, where they even spread to New England during the Salem witch trials. Estimates of the number of executions over these centuries range from tens of thousands to over *nine million*.[13] While men were also tried, the main victims of the witch-hunts were women, particularly older women,[14] rightfully deeming this by feminists and scholars to be the "Women's Holocaust."

Why did the Church target older women—the Crone aspect of the Triple Goddess—in particular? Older women had acted—like Brigid—as the community midwives, seers, and healers. Beyond concocting remedies to ease labor pains, these Wise Women could help younger women with natural birth control and even abortion, which was in direct conflict with the Church's values. By giving power over their sexual and reproductive choices to women, the Wise Women threatened the Church's ability to exercise control over women's bodies, sexuality, and their most intimate life choices.

Scholars also point out that women who were most targeted were those who defied or lived outside of patriarchal norms and preferred solitary and independent lives while serving the poor with their healing gifts.[15]

Moreover, as the Church meant to act as the intermediary between the people and their heavenly Father

---

13   Dr. Susan Greenwood, *Witchcraft: A History* (Lorenz Books) 121.

14   Brian P. Levack, *The Witch-Hunt in Early Modern Europe* (Routledge) 129.

15   Steven T. Katz, *The Holocaust in Historical Context*, Volume 1 (Oxford University Press, 1994) 468–69.

God, the Wise Woman's ability to connect with the Divine directly through her intuition and Mother Goddess on earth further undermined the Church.

Women's spiritual crafts—or witchcraft—was our way of harnessing the natural powers and spirits of the elements and cosmos and the Divine powers within ourselves. As contemporary witch and author Starhawk says in *The Spiral Dance*, "In the Craft, we do not believe in the Goddess—we connect with Her; through the moon, the stars, the ocean, the earth, through trees, animals, through other human beings, through ourselves. She is here. She is within us all."[16]

But under the Church's targeted campaign against witches, the sacred practices that came naturally to these women became punishable acts of devil worship. Where once even Brigid's symbols as Goddess were Her protective cloak, cauldron, and healing herbs, now women using these magical tools were persecuted as witches.

Where locals were once free to celebrate the eight Sabbats of the Goddess's Wheel of the Year, (beginning with Brigid's own holy day of Imbolc on February 1), the Church began charging people with heresy and witchery for honoring these holy days.

It continued its campaign to deem women who worked with and gathered in nature as

16   Starhawk, *The Spiral Dance: A Rebirth of the Ancient Religion of the Goddess* (New York: HarperCollins Publishers, 1979).

Satan-worshipers, accusing them of having sex and conspiring with the devil to bring plagues and all forms of evil to the locals. Void of reason and desperate for someone to blame for all the calamities that befell them, neighbors conspired against neighbors, and entire communities witnessed and partook in the female genocide that went on for centuries.

The eventual rise of modern rationalism, science, and the Enlightenment Era around the mid-seventeenth to early eighteenth centuries finally brought the decline and eventual end of the long and horrific era of the witch-hunts.

Nevertheless, those of us who have been tried, tortured, and executed as Wise Women in past lives may still struggle with releasing the deeply encoded fears of activating and especially sharing our gifts. In my coaching practice, so many of my highly-gifted clients come to me because they wish to serve others with their innate healing abilities, but they can't get past their fear of "coming out" spiritually.

Without exception, in our work together we always uncover a past life in which they were persecuted for their spiritual beliefs and abilities. Out of self-preservation, they ended up carrying a deep-rooted fear of showcasing this side of themselves so that they can remain unseen and therefore safe. Thankfully, we are able to release these karmic codes, and my beloved clients are able to build flourishing practices that deeply fulfill them and support others with their gifts.

But I completely understand and relate to their fears. Before I could feel safe and empowered enough to go public with my healing work in this life, I myself had to re-script memories of being hunted and burned as a witch when I was a recluse healer in a past life.

I also learned firsthand how deeply lodged past-life traumas can get into our cellular memories. In my regression, I had seen my last boss as one of my persecutors, which was not a surprise given our relationship in this lifetime. A year into my practice, my husband ran into her and proudly updated her on my career change. Later that same day, my body broke out into a severe, mysterious reaction—one I had never had before nor have had since. *I actually felt like it was on fire.*

As I tuned into my body, I immediately saw a vision of my old boss spewing slimy, green, venomous energy at me. She almost looked like a demon having a tantrum. When I meditated on what I needed to learn from this, my soul revealed that my old boss's unconscious, past-life self became enraged as she confronted the fact that she no longer held any power over me.

Not just that, but her fury at hearing that I was freely practicing and flourishing as a healer triggered the memories in my own body of being burned by her. Of course, I cleared and shielded myself and cut any remaining cords with her so that we could both be free on our journeys.

But I share this with you, my sister, because I know

that whether or not you too have had a past life in which you were condemned and punished for your spiritual gifts, that simply by virtue of being a woman, you share in the collective unconscious imprint. We all bear the energetic scars left by centuries of witch-hunts and the degradation of the Goddess that started with the rise of patriarchal reign long before. The memories of these personal or collective wounds can still get triggered in your present day life as you commit to exploring, honing, and especially sharing your Wise Woman gifts.

Our spiritual gifts have been feared and punished because they are rooted in our natural, personal, spiritual connection to the Divine that is beyond the confines and control of oppressive structures or ordained intermediaries. Witchcraft is women's wisdom, and it is a sacred rite we need to reclaim.

We conjure our witchy gifts from our direct, intimate connection with the Goddess, Mother Earth, and our own Sacred Feminine mysteries. Our sexuality, our intuition, our resourcefulness, our rightful wrath, our menstrual cycles, our healing gifts, our compassion, our creative *shakti*—these are all forces of *our nature* that are our sacred right to fearlessly own—whether we are revered as Wise Women or burned as witches for doing so.

When we re-learn

> *We Wise Women conjure our witchy gifts from our direct, intimate connection with the Goddess, Mother Earth, and our own Sacred Feminine mysteries.*

the rituals and practices that honored our connection with the Goddess, we awaken the natural magic that is within and all around us. We harness the powers of the earth, moon, and cosmos. We work reverently with the elements. We connect intimately with the Divine. We channel messages and miracles from Spirit. We replace rigid religious instruction with intuitive spiritual experience, whether it comes to us through dance, song, ritual, or heart-prayer. We bring heaven down to earth. We make the mundane sacred and the sinful blessed.

It is time now, my sister, to reclaim *your* inner Wise Woman, to heal the witch wound, and resurrect your Goddess-given gifts that are so needed in our world. Know that when you do this work, you heal yourself and all the women and men who share in our collective wounding.

By resurrecting Brigid within, you heal the encoding of oppression in your karmic history, your family lineage, your future generations, and all us women through all of time.

It seems Brigid, in Her wisdom, saw the times to come and found a way to survive as a Goddess disguised as a Saint so that She may continue to support Her daughters and people.

She stands ready with you now to give you back your magical tools and powers. Claim them.

As you move forward on your path, Brigid will be the guide who is ever ready to share Her own sacred fire to support and protect you through any stage of healing and transformation.

And the truth is, so long as we are committed to embracing the full experience of our life and the higher desire of our soul to grow, we will always be in a state of transmutation in some aspect of our lives. Welcome it, beloved, knowing that Brigid within will always light the way.

PRE-INITIATION PREPARATION:

- Light a red, orange, or green candle at your altar.

- Play relaxing Celtic music in the background.

BRIGID'S INITIATION: RECLAIMING YOUR INNER WISE WOMAN
Ritual Type: Guided Meditation

Sitting comfortably in meditation, close your eyes. Gently focus on your breath, centering in the rhythm of its inflow and outflow. Simultaneously bring your awareness to your third eye, in the middle of your forehead, and in the pit of your belly.

If it's comfortable for you, let your exhales be slightly louder and longer than your inhales, connecting with the fiery power of your solar plexus *chakra*.

Imagining a bubble of golden light encompassing you, feel or see yourself lifted up, above your room and then beyond this space, into the sacred inner realms.

Your bubble comes to a stop, and you step outside. You find yourself standing at Brigid's mystical temple in ancient Cill Dara, Ireland, (now known as Kildare). As you take in the magical energy of this land, you are greeted by nineteen priestesses who tend to Brigid's sacred flame, which burns eternally in the inner realms.

As they welcome you in, you begin to walk with them in a spiraling labyrinth of three holy circles, honoring Brigid's Triple Goddess nature.

You now arrive at the center and witness Her flame burning bright. Its fiery dance is hypnotic, and you find yourself entering into a deep, divine trance as you watch the flames. Slowly, you see Brigid emerge from Her sacred fire.

She is delighted to see you, Her sister and daughter, and embraces you with a deeply nourishing and fiercely protective maternal love. You melt into Her arms, feeling an ancient connection awaken within your heart, womb, blood, and bones.

"Welcome back, my beloved sister, my cherished daughter," She says. "It is time to remember the Wise Woman ways and reclaim your spiritual powers."

She guides you to look into Her sacred fire and begins to show you visions of priestesses, shamans, medicine women, midwives, healers, seers, and witches living in oneness with Mother Earth and fully awakened to and practicing their spiritual crafts. You see women from all cultures and times doing this sacred work, safely and freely.

Witnessing these Wise Women begins to stir your

own past-life memories, and knowing this, Brigid intuitively shows you these lifetimes.

First, She reveals lifetimes where you freely and safely honed and practiced your spiritual gifts. Notice what you did. Sense where you were. Feel the joy and magic that was a natural way of being for you as you lived and served from your full spiritual power. What were the commitments you made to yourself about honoring your spirituality? About serving others through your soul's journey?

See the miracles and blessings you channeled for yourself and others, whether it was for your family, sisterhood, or community.

Keeping these empowering memories in your conscious awareness, Brigid now amplifies the fiery light inside your belly, and gives you a flaming sword of light. If and only if you feel ready, She begins to reveal to you lifetimes in which it was not safe for you to practice your ways.

Notice who you were and what you believed and practiced. Notice the times. Witness what happened. What did others do? What did you do? How did you feel? How did you react or respond? What were the fear-based conclusions that you made about your spirituality as a result of these experiences?

Keeping you strong and steady, Brigid uses Her flame to draw out memories from your cellular DNA so that you may see the lingering effects of these self-sabotaging and fear-based beliefs. As you purge the stored pain and darkness of these unconscious memories, Brigid throws them into Her fire, where they are instantly burned, cleared, and transmuted.

With your flaming sword, you cut all cords and ties to these memories. You keep only the lesson of taking back your Goddess-given power and your sacred right to live from it always and fully.

Her priestesses join you in sacred circle and begin to channel and purge the painful memories from all Wise Women, through all of time, including and especially the witch-hunts. The condemnation and oppression of all women is now thrown into Brigid's fire, where it is instantly and completely healed and transformed.

As you and the fellow priestesses release all fear of us women collectively living in our full Sacred Feminine power, Brigid's fire turns into an iridescent gold. This is the light of Wise Women's alchemical power, which now courses through your veins. It continues to heal, cleanse, and transmute you and spreads to all women through all of time, filling and encircling them with Divine protection.

The light ignites your forehead, like Brigid's own ascending flame, and re-initiates you into your spiritual sight of divination, intuition, and prophecy.

The light now ignites your hands, re-initiating you into your natural gifts of healing touch and creative expression.

The light shines through your throat, re-initiating you into your powers as oracle and guide.

The light flows through your womb, re-initiating you as a medicine woman, herbal healer, and midwife.

The light shines through your core, re-initiating you into the Warrior Goddess–Crone power you need to blaze forward as you re-forge your path, ignited with your spiritual powers.

The light flows through your entire body, re-initiating you into the clear vessel of Divine love and miracles that are in your truth.

As you look around your circle, you see that your own initiation has healed and re-initiated all the women who came before you and the women who will come after you into their own Divine Feminine wisdom and power.

You all bow to each other in reverence. You know that it is safe and right for you and all women to now reclaim our feminine wisdom for ourselves, our families, our communities, our Mother Earth, and our world.

Our healing, our love, and our light are needed now more than ever. And we are ready to rise. You are ready to rise.

With Brigid's blessing, you have now transformed beyond and transcended your Wise Woman wounds and are ready to shine and flourish in all ways.

Brigid offers you even more protection by shielding you in layered cloaks of fiery golden light, which will continue to transmute any darkness sent your way so that you may feel and be safe to practice and share your crafts once again.

As you let your Divine light shine as brightly as a splendid sun, you see all your fellow sisters. With us all shining, the circle clears.

Thanking Brigid and your fellow priestess sisters, you begin to make your journey back, holding Brigid's flame in hand.

Brigid kisses your hands and forehead, further awakening your magical gifts, and lovingly brings you back to Mother Earth, fully into your own body temple now.

Keeping your awareness on your belly and third eye, you bring your palms together, and rub your hands together as fast you can for thirty-three seconds. When done, immediately place your left hand on your forehead and right on your belly.

Feel the healing warmth of your hands flow through your third eye and solar plexus *chakras* and know that you can give yourself this healing touch whenever you need.

Feeling re-centered in your Wise Woman wisdom and power, slowly open your eyes, beloved.

Blow out Brigid's candle and drink fresh spring water to aid the clearing effects of this initiation.

POST-INITIATION SELF-CARE:

- Write a letter of any painful memories or fears that came up during your initiation, and safely burn it in a cauldron or steel or iron pot. Wash away the ashes, allowing Brigid's sacred waters to cleanse them.

- Take a shower and imagine Brigid's healing well waters further cleansing and replenishing you.

- Place your hands anywhere on your body that needs more healing love and imagine golden light flowing through.

- Dance to festive Celtic music to ground and celebrate your re-initiation, and envision and feel Wise Women from all of time dancing freely and blissfully with you!

Affirming Brigid:

Call me a witch or a crone
Burn me down to the bone
The fire you use is my domain
Through its ashes I will rise again.

My eternal flame will forge anew
A golden sword of power true
My sisters and I will blaze the path
For wise women to rise, hand-in-hand.

I Am Brigid.

Goddess Brigid

Origin: Celtic

Also Called: Brid, Bride, Bighde, Brigantia, Brigandu, Brig, Brighid, and Saint Brigit

Name Meanings: Bright Arrow, The Bright One, The Fiery Arrow, The Powerful One, The High One, Bright Lady, Lady of the Shores

Attributes:

- Triple Goddess (Maiden, Mother, Crone)
- Alchemy
- Magic
- Manifesting
- Miracles
- Healing
- Fertility
- Midwifery
- Mothering
- Nurturing
- Wisdom
- Divination
- Creativity
- Writing, especially poetry
- Music
- Art
- Hearth/warmth
- Blacksmithing
- Courage

- Protection
- Transformation
- Transmutation
- Success

Sacred Symbols:

- Fire, particularly the flame
- Sun
- Wells
- Milk
- Quill or pen
- Arrow
- Sword
- Cauldron
- Chalice
- Cloak
- Wand
- Ox
- Cow
- Sheep
- Boar
- Serpent
- Moon (all phases)
- Herbs

Chakras:

- Solar Plexus
- Third eye
- Sacral
- Heart

Elements:

- Fire
- Water

Essential Oils:

- Lavender
- Cinnamon
- Ginger
- Rosemary
- Juniper
- Geranium

Colors:

- Red
- Orange
- Yellow
- Gold
- White
- Green

Crystals:

- Citrine
- Clear quartz
- Emerald
- Gold (metal)
- Red jasper
- Tiger's eye (orange and red)

Archetype in Balance:

- Wise
- Intuitive
- Magical
- Creative
- Inspired
- Empowered
- Courageous
- Clear
- Focused
- Confident

- Optimistic
- Decisive
- Nurturing
- Service-oriented
- Purpose-driven
- Connected to the earth
- Connected to Spirit
- Centered in personal and spiritual power
- Self-aware
- Can take responsibility for personal growth and healing
- Inspires and empowers others through personal example
- Welcomes transformation
- Is comfortable in and enjoys solitude

Archetype out of Balance:

- Has difficulty receiving intuitive guidance
- Doesn't trust and follow inner guidance
- Stagnant
- Uninspired
- Gives power away
- Insecure
- Confused
- Lacks focus
- Aggressive
- Martyr
- Tries to rescue others
- Has spiritual ego
- Ungrounded
- Can isolate self
- Projects onto others
- Doesn't take responsibility for personal wounds

- Lacks self-awareness

- Resists pain and growth

- Hides spiritual side out of fear of judgment or condemnation

- Can have social anxiety

- Can misuse spiritual power (to condemn, control, or punish others)

Creating Balance:

- Welcome healing and transformation as part of your spiritual path and personal evolution.

- Explore the healing arts.

- Hone your spiritual gifts.

- Share your spiritual, healing, and creative gifts.

- Use oracles, meditation, and divination to receive spiritual guidance.

- Work with the natural elements to create more harmony and magic in your life.

- Offer yourself as a vessel of love and miracles.

- Summon your inner Warrioress to honor your path.

- Don't be afraid of judgment, especially with your spirituality.

- Own your "woo-woo," because the world needs it.

- Use fire in ritual (smudging, burning letters of what you want to release).

- Use water for healing (herbal baths, steams).

- Use herbs for healing and magic (as teas, tinctures, essential oils, Bach Flower remedies).

- Meditate and ground yourself daily.

- Take responsibility for your own healing.

- Nurture yourself through sacred self-care.

- Connect with like-minded community

- Reclaim your spiritual power.

- Be the authority in your life.

- Balance alone time with loving, fulfilling, and honoring relationships.

- Use your spiritual power for everyone's highest good.

Associated Goddesses:

- Hecate (Greek)

- Isis (Egyptian)

- Spider Woman (Native American)

- Morgaine le Fay (Celtic)

- Saraswati (Indian)

- Kuan Yin (Chinese/Buddhist)

Prayer/Invocation:

Beloved Brigid, as Goddess of alchemy within me, I welcome the fires of your flame to transmute all that no longer serves me on my path to being a clear channel of miracles for myself and others.

Ignite my own Divine spark of inspiration and creation so that I may manifest magical blessings and inspire others to do the same. Grant me the courage to fully embrace and share my spiritual wisdom and gifts.

Let me forge the way for us women to reclaim our Sacred Feminine mysteries, healing myself and all sisters before me, and all sisters to come after me. So be it. So it is.

Gateway 13

TAKING YOUR THRONE

INITIATOR:
ISIS, GODDESS OF ALL

Isis

MIGHTY ONE,
FOREMOST OF THE GODDESSES
RULER IN HEAVEN,
QUEEN ON EARTH…
ALL THE DEITIES
ARE UNDER HER COMMAND.
—INSCRIPTION TO ISIS AT PHILAE

My beloved, here you are. Here you are. Awakened to your feminine wisdom and power by the grace of all the Goddesses you have activated within you on this journey.

It is time now, my sister, to take your rightful throne so that you may sit as the Sovereign Queen in the center of your life.

Initiating you on your final, most blessed step is the Queen Goddess of all Herself, the adored and venerated Egyptian Goddess Isis. Her Kemetic (ancient Egyptian) name *Auset* or *Ast* means "throne," and Her hieroglyphic sign is also the throne, for She is ruler of all Gods and Goddesses in heaven and of all kings and queens on earth. She is the very personification of the Divine and regal power of the throne.

Beyond the throne, as Goddess of Ten Thousand names, Isis is the culmination and embodiment

Isis is **all of you: *dark and light, human and Divine, woman and Goddess.***

of *all Sacred Feminine powers* you have awakened on your journey thus far, and all that you ever will after. As Isis-Panthea, She is the "All Goddess," the fullest expression of your Divine nature alchemized and actualized.

She is here to remind you that it is time to take the lead in your life and become an empowered, wise, abundant, and loving Queen in your domain and in the world. She is here to show you that as Goddess of all Goddesses, She is *all of you*: dark and light, human and Divine, woman and Goddess.

Her all-encompassing nature is expressed through Her countless names, hymns inscribed on Her sacred temples, and ancient texts that have been translated by devotees and scholars alike for thousands of years. The truth of Her sacred words has the power to awaken and affirm your own nature as Queen Goddess of all, and I hope as you read the passages below that they do.

For when you know yourself as Isis, you are in essence simultaneously invoking all the Goddesses you have met individually. You are weaving all their gifts within the tapestry of your own essence, consciously embodying and expressing the full spectrum of your Divine Feminine nature.

ISIS AS GODDESS OF SILENCE

One of Isis's names in the Egyptian *Book of the Dead* is

"Lover of silence."[17] Like Sige, She is also associated with the Goddess of knowledge and wisdom, Sophia, and in this form She is even called Isis-Sophia.

In "The Thunder, Perfect Mind," a Coptic text incorporated into the Gnostic *Nag Hammadi*, Isis-Sophia affirms Herself as "the silence that is incomprehensible and the idea whose remembrance is frequent."[18]

Isis is the empty presence through which you will continue to receive, conceive, and birth your Divine wisdom as you move forward. She is the idea of your own Divine self whose remembrance is as frequent as you connect with it in sacred stillness.

She is the voice of the soul of the universe speaking through your own soul, through outer signs and inner guidance. She is the word of the Divine and of truth, which appears to you in endless ways, so that you may connect in ways that most speak to *your* soul.

> *Isis is the empty presence through which you receive, conceive, and birth your Divine wisdom.*

Isis is the sacred mystery that is accessible to us all. She is the guidance that is to be

---

17   E.A. Wallis Budge, *The Book of the Dead*, (Publication of 1895 based on the *Papyrus of Ani* in possession of the British Museum) 1895.
18   George W. MacRae, "The Thunder, Perfect Mind," *Nag Hammadi*, Codex VI, Tractate 2: Protocol of the Fifth Colloquy (1973) The Center for Hermeneutical Studies in Hellenistic and Modern Culture, 1975.

felt through the heart and known through the soul, which cannot be comprehended through the mind alone.

As ancient Greek high priest and scribe Plutarch shared with a priestess of Delphi (first century AD), Isis "discloses the Divine mysteries to those who truly and justly have the name of 'bearers of the sacred vessels' and 'wearers of the sacred robes.'"[19]

When you robe yourself in solitude and silence the voice in your mind, you open the chambers of your soul, inviting Divine wisdom to enter and fill you. You become, as a High Priestess, the vessel for the Goddess to flow through you.

Isis, like Sige, is the essence of silence, and the great void through which all is birthed. She gently implores you to access Her wisdom through a conscious, daily practice of stillness. For only in silence can She speak to you clearly. And only in stillness can you perceive Her mysteries.

ISIS AS THE GODDESS OF HEAVEN AND THE UNDERWORLD

Isis is also here to solidify your initiation with the next Goddesses you met after Sige, for She is Queen of heaven,

---

19   Plutarch, *Moralia*, vol. 5, trans. Frank Cole Babbitt (Loeb Classical Library edition, 1936).

earth, and the underworld. As She proclaims to Her devotee Lucius in his tale, *The Metamorphosis*, Isis is "the sovereign of the spirits of the dead, the first of the celestials."[20]

She is the one who rules "the luminous summits of the heavens, the salubrious breezes of the sea, and the deplorable silences of the realms beneath."[21]

She is your spirit and your shadow, your human grief and your Divine power. She needs you to see your light and dark. For Isis knows the pangs of grief and is a Goddess of mourning and lamentation Herself. Like Ereshkigal who bit Her lip and slapped Her thigh when Inanna entered Her domain, Isis cut Her hair and tore Her clothes when She heard of Her beloved husband Osiris's death by Their jealous brother Set.

In the *Egyptian Book of the Dead*, it is said that when She set out to search for His body, Isis "wandered round and round the earth uttering cries of pain, and She rested not until She had found Him."

Her tears flooded the Nile every spring, inundating and fertilizing the desert lands to create new life from death, as Inanna arose anew from Hers. Both Goddess myths of descending into the underworld and ascending

Isis is the power to be found through the wisdom in your wounds.

---

20   Apuleius, *The Metamorphosis, or The Golden Ass, and Philosophical Works of Apuleius*, trans. Thomas Taylor (London: Sold by R. Triphook and T. Rodd, 1822).

21   Ibid.

into new life honor the cycles of death, healing, resurrection, and renewal that we too are initiated into through the seasons of our lives and in our very own cyclical nature as women.

Isis is the power to be found through the wisdom in your wounds. And She asks once again that you embrace and not forsake their gifts, beloved. She wants you to take your throne as you delve below into Ereshkigal, Queen of the underworld (your unconscious, shadow self), and revere Her equally as you come up to sit on your heavenly throne (your conscious, spiritual self) as Inanna. Only then can you be the rightful ruler of your whole self.

ISIS AS THE GODDESS OF TRANSFORMATION

Isis, as Lady of heat and fire and Lady of lightning, comes to you next as the lava fires of Pele's wrath, which you will continue to erupt when rightfully called for. For She is both the "control and the uncontrollable" and the "union and the dissolution."[22]

Isis knows that sometimes unleashing disruptive forces is the only way to clear what no longer serves you and fertilize the lava-enriched soils for new beginnings.

22   George W. MacRae, "The Thunder, Perfect Mind," *Nag Hammadi*, Codex VI, Tractate 2: Protocol of the Fifth Colloquy (1973) The Center for Hermeneutical Studies in Hellenistic and Modern Culture, 1975.

She is the Divine Feminine *shakti* within you that is yours to wield at your will—to unleash for destruction of the old and creation of the new.

Just as Pele is the Goddess of unrestrained forces like lava and lightning, Isis is the unbridled harbinger of transformation. In addition to being the Mistress of all elements, Isis has powerful tools at Her disposal to shake up old foundations, one of which was Her magical *sistrum* (ancient Egyptian rattle). As Plutarch shares, "The sistrum also makes it clear that all things in existence need to be shaken, or rattled about, and never to cease from motion but, as it were, to be waked up and agitated when they grow drowsy and torpid."

Like Pele's erupting volcanoes, Isis knows that sometimes unleashing disruptive forces is the only way to clear what no longer serves you and fertilize the lava-enriched soils for new beginnings.

Both Goddesses invite you to own your sacred rage as you move forward so that you may cleanse your life and clear the way, dancing like Pele and Isis in rapture and with abandon.

ISIS AS THE GODDESS OF POWER

Isis now affirms your inner Kali, to continue to liberate and empower you. Her names as the Mighty One,

Protectress, Savioress, and Goddess of war are your own Divine powers to overcome your greatest inner and outer foes.

While men have long been ascribed the role of protector, Isis reminds women that we hold the power to protect ourselves, our children, and our men. In the *Book of the Dead*, She is credited for Her role in protecting not only Her son Horus as a single mother, but even Her God-king husband Osiris: "Thy sister put forth Her protecting power for thee, She scattered abroad those who were Her enemies."

Like Kali *Ma*, Isis is the fiercely protective Mother, for She had to protect Her son Horus from Her brother Set, who sought to murder the holy child as He did Osiris. She went through many harsh trials of Her own, each one testing the bounds of Her strength. But as She always persevered, each test elevated Isis to a new level of Her own Divine strength, wisdom, and power.

As one who has transcended tragedy and trial, Isis knows the necessity of harsh transformation. She reminds you that whatever trials life sends your way, know that each one is an invitation to a higher initiation on your spiritual path. For only in the taking away and tearing down of all that you hold dear can you come to

Isis as your inner Warrioress helps you overcome all that stands in the way of your liberation and highest self-realization.

know your true self. No matter how much you resist, She will sever all your attachments to align you back with your truth out of Her love for you. You can count on it.

And yet, Isis knows what it is like to be afraid in the face of adversity, for She is the one who "exists in all fears and (is) strength in trembling."[23] As you tremble with fear when facing the obstacles before you or demons within you, Isis as Kali is your own inner Warrioress, summoning your bloodlust and screaming out your battle-cry to overcome all that stands in the way of your liberation and highest self-realization.

ISIS AS THE GODDESS OF COMPASSION

And when you are done with your battling and just need a soft place to fall, Isis is Kuan Yin as the Sacred Feminine gift of compassion within you, just as She appears to the desperate character Lucius in his moment of crisis, lovingly assuring him: "Behold, Lucius, I, moved by thy tears, am

You lead with grace in the world when you offer the grace of compassion to yourself first.

---

23 George W. MacRae, "The Thunder, Perfect Mind," *Nag Hammadi*, Codex VI, Tractate 2: Protocol of the Fifth Colloquy (1973) The Center for Hermeneutical Studies in Hellenistic and Modern Culture, 1975.

present with thee (...) I, commiserating thy calamities, I am present, favoring and propitious. Dismiss now your tears and lamentations, and expel sorrow. Now, through my providence, the salutary day will shine upon thee."[24]

Like Kuan Yin, Isis is She who hears all prayers, here to remind you that you are never alone in your suffering, beloved. She reminds you that as Sovereign Queen, you will lead with grace in the world when you offer the grace of compassion to yourself and call in Divine support through your heart-prayers.

Isis knows the pains of healing, and like Kuan Yin with Her *amrita* waters, Isis cleanses your heart with Her holy Nile waters. She knows it is the waters of your tears (like Her own) that will revive your soul and spring forth new sprouts of love and blessings in your life.

ISIS AS THE GODDESS OF LOVE

Love, too, is Isis's domain, for She herself says to Lucius, "on Cyprus they call me golden Aphrodite."[25]

As Aphrodite within you, She is the source of

---

24 Apuleius, *The Metamorphosis, or The Golden Ass, and Philosophical Works of Apuleius*, trans. Thomas Taylor (London: Sold by R. Triphook and T. Rodd, 1822).

25 Ibid..

Divine love, radiant beauty, sacred sexuality, and ecstatic pleasure. And She knows the price we women pay as we dare to embrace these gifts as She herself has been called both "the whore and the holy one." [26]

Isis as your inner Aphrodite sweetly beckons you to love your body and honor your soul so that you may be the holy vessel of endless pleasures, merging all the delights of heaven and earth through your beautiful body temple. She reminds you that you are both sexual and sacred, and you have a sovereign right to experience yourself as both.

Her names attribute Her as simultaneously being the Divine Wife and the Great Virgin. Isis is you as the lover who embraces sacred sexual union. She is the devoted and loyal wife/partner who allows Herself to be cherished and ravished by Her beloved. And She is also your self-sufficiency and wholeness, which is yours independent of your relationships.

As Queen-Goddess wife to King-God Osiris, who miraculously conceived their holy child Horus, Isis's union with Her beloved also represents the inner mystical marriage of God-Goddess, and the miracles you birth forth

You are both sexual and sacred, and you have a sovereign right to experience yourself as both.

---

26   George W. MacRae, "The Thunder, Perfect Mind," *Nag Hammadi*, Codex VI, Tractate 2: Protocol of the Fifth Colloquy (1973) The Center for Hermeneutical Studies in Hellenistic and Modern Culture, 1975.

---

from this. When you love and embrace all of yourself, you unite yourself into sacred wholeness and become the vessel for birthing the Divine through you on earth.

Aphrodite too birthed Her holy child, Eros, god of romantic love, through Her union with Ares, Her Divine Masculine counterpart. When you merge all the polarities within yourself, their sacred union creates miraculous new expressions of Divine love, within and without.

And you, as a woman, as a Goddess, are the Divine Feminine vessel required for the Divine Masculine (consciousness) to manifest into form. *You* are the Goddess of love. And love begets miraculous creations.

LOVE AS EXPRESSED THROUGH BEAUTY

Love is beautiful, and as a Goddess, you are the embodiment and bringer of beauty. Isis as Lady of love and Lady of beauty taught women many spiritual and earthly arts, one of which was beautification. In Her colored hieroglyphics (that I was blessed to see for myself during a trip to Egypt), seeing Isis adorned with beautiful makeup, regal clothing, and exquisite jewels is a vision to behold. She is, after all, the Queen Goddess within who compels us to treat ourselves as the worthy and beautiful empresses that we truly are.

For us sensitive, soulful women, it can be easy to invest our time and energy in our spirits. But Isis and

Aphrodite remind you that your body is the temple of your spirit. And just as their temples were made and cared for with deep love, reverence, and beauty, they compel you to treat your body the same way. Let this aspect of your inner Isis and Aphrodite empower you to pamper and beautify yourself with joy and without guilt.

These Goddesses also inspire you to bring more beauty into your outer world. Whether it is through fresh flowers, a work of art, sensuous fabrics, magical crystals, or scented candles, take time to delight your senses and your soul through the Sacred Feminine gift of beauty.

LOVE AS THE ULTIMATE HEALER

Isis knows and shows that love is the most healing and powerful force of all. Isis searched far and wide across foreign lands to find the body of Her beloved Osiris after Set murdered Him. When Set learned that Isis had found the coffin containing Osiris's body, He repossessed it and then severed the body into fourteen pieces, scattering the late king's dismembered parts into the Nile.

Isis, with the help of Her sister (and wife of Set) Nephthys, once again embarked on a treacherous search for Osiris's body parts. Through loving determination,

They retrieved and tied back together all but one piece: His penis, which was eaten by a fish.

Never one to be deterred, Isis fashioned a sacred new phallus for Her beloved out of pure gold. She then began to fervently chant spells and dance around His body so vigorously that Her arms spread into wings, and their beating breathed life back into Osiris. As shared in *The Book of the Dead*, Isis "overshadowed Him with Her feathers, She made wind with Her wings, and She uttered cries at the burial of Her brother."

The revival was short-lived but lasted just long enough for the Divine couple to make love one last time. Through the magic of Her love, Isis, "raised up the prostrate form of Him whose heart was still, She took from Him of His essence, She conceived and brought forth a child."[27] Through this final union, Isis miraculously conceived Their son Horus, who would go on to avenge His father, restore Isis upon Her throne, and become the just and rightful king of Upper and Lower Egypt.

Like Isis, Aphrodite too lost her beloved Adonis when he pursued a dangerous hunt after the Goddess's pleas for him not to, and he was tragically killed by a wild boar. As Aphrodite held Her deceased lover in Her arms, in Her mourning,

Through the power of love, even the deepest heartbreak can be healed, and the greatest tragedies can be transformed.

---

27   E.A. Wallis Budge, *The Book of the Dead*, (Publication of 1895 based on the *Papyrus of Ani* in possession of the British Museum) 1895.

She turned the blood that dripped from his lifeless body into bright red anemone flowers.

Both Goddesses remind us that through the power of love, even the deepest heartbreak can be healed, and the greatest tragedies can be transformed. This alchemical elixir is the endless source of Divine love within you, beloved. You can always draw on it for your own restoration and renewal, no matter what your heart goes through as you open it to the joys and pains of loving.

ISIS AS THE GODDESS OF WISHES

Isis is also your highest hopes and dreams, as is the wish-fulfilling Tara. Her names Isis-Sothis and Isis-Sopdet connected the Goddess to the star we know as Sirius and in which form She was depicted with a star upon Her crown. The resurgence of Sirius in the spring marked the inundation of the Nile and beginning of a new year, one pregnant with renewed hope and promise.

Just as Tara inspired you with Divine visions for your soul's dreams, Isis invites you to align your hopes with the brightest of all the stars: Sirius. She is the light of your heart's highest aspirations. She is the brilliance of your soul's greatest expression. Whenever you set standards for your life and affirm your Divine dreams, shoot for nothing less than the brightest of all of heaven's stars as is befitting for the Queen that you are.

And, like Tara, Isis offers you Her complete protection as you shine your brightest light and live your most glorious life. She says as much to you as She did to Lucius, "You will live happy, you will live glorious, under my protection."[28]

ISIS AS THE GODDESS OF WISDOM

To help you take inspired action to co-create your starry dreams into earthly manifestation, Isis will guide you as your inner wisdom, as your inner Athena. Plutarch described Isis as "a Goddess exceptionally wise and a lover of wisdom, to whom, as Her name at least seems to indicate, knowledge and understanding are in the highest degree appropriate."[29]

Isis, like Athena, gave Her people the practical tools for agriculture, civilization, law and order, commerce, language, and seamanship. Her many attributes connecting Her to Athena are expressed in Her names as Queen of seamanship, justice,

---

28   Apuleius, *The Metamorphosis, or The Golden Ass, and Philosophical Works of Apuleius*, trans. Thomas Taylor (London: Sold by R. Triphook and T. Rodd, 1822).

29   Plutarch, *Moralia*, vol. 5, trans. Frank Cole Babbitt (Loeb Classical Library edition, 1936).

lawmaker, knowledge, wisdom, understanding, inventor, Goddess of literature, Goddess of women, Lady of the weaving, and Lady of peace, to name just a few.

Isis is as much a Goddess of esoteric knowledge and magic as She is a patron of strategic planning and practical action. For She knows firsthand that a powerful Queen has to be both. To ensure that you succeed in all your inspired endeavors, Isis as your inner Athena will lovingly encourage you to trust and follow your intuition with joyful, focused, and disciplined action.

She knows that as a woman, you may seek and consider the guidance of those you respect. But She reminds you that while a Queen may have many advisers, ultimately she must seek no council outside of herself when making her decisions and honoring her path.

ISIS AS THE GODDESS OF FREEDOM

To keep you soaring high and free on your path, Isis will give you wings as Lilith did in your initiation with Her. She knows and proudly accepts the consequences of being the Wild Woman who is scorned and shunned

Isis enchants you into living with sacred lust for life—from the **shakti** *fire that erupts from your holy loins.*

for honoring Her deepest desires, for She proclaims Herself as the one who is both lust and self-control, sinless and the source of sin, and both scorned and venerated.[30]

Isis enchants you into living with sacred lust for life—from the *shakti* fire that erupts from your holy loins. Be the Queen that lives fully and truly. Pay no heed to those who may judge or condemn you. For Isis reminds you that the true sin is self-denial and the greatest punishment is self-betrayal. So spread your wings and fly high, inspiring others to join you if they wish.

Isis also compels you to speak your truth with conviction so that you may honor your values and command the respect you deserve as a woman, as a Queen, and as a Goddess. As She is credited in the *Book of the Dead*, Isis could dispatch those who sought to wrong Her through the power and conviction of Her words and voice: "She drove back evil hap, She pronounced mighty words of power, She made cunning Her tongue, and Her words failed not. The glorious Isis was perfect in command and in speech."

Whenever someone dares to encroach on your sacred boundaries, invoke the authoritative voice of your inner Lilith and Isis to take a stand for your sovereign rights.

---

30   George W. MacRae, "The Thunder, Perfect Mind," *Nag Hammadi*, Codex VI, Tractate 2: Protocol of the Fifth Colloquy (1973) The Center for Hermeneutical Studies in Hellenistic and Modern Culture, 1975.

ISIS AS THE GODDESS OF WOMB WISDOM

To support you in honoring the cycles of your path and your own Divine Feminine nature, Isis next blesses you as Yemanya within. Isis too is Goddess of the moon and seas, and embodies the Maiden-Mother-Crone powers of conception, creation, and transformation within your womb.

As both Divine Daughter and Mother of the Gods, like Yemanya, Isis is both the innocent receptivity of the Maiden and the creative *shakti* of the Mother.

In "The Thunder, Perfect Mind," Isis describes Herself as being both fertile and barren. Isis is the hopes and dreams that have not yet come to be, or perhaps are not meant to be. She is the countless creations you have already birthed, and the all that is yet to be.

I, myself, have desired to become a mother for quite some time now, and the journey has been one of the greatest initiations of my life. I am both comforted and frustrated by the knowledge that physically my husband and I are very healthy and fertile. And after doing "all the right things" to get pregnant, through deep, painful spiritual work, I have finally come to trust that this has nothing to do with

Isis is the countless creations you have already birthed and the all that is yet to be.

our bodies. I know now that this is a matter of Divine wisdom and timing and not something that we can control or force physically.

Yet I also understand that when we aren't able to manifest what we desire in spite of our best efforts, it is natural for us to feel barren and even betrayed by the Divine in that area of our lives. And I know all too well the profound pain this can bring us. It is why I continue to hold Ereshkigal with such reverence as we have become intimate friends on a journey where the Goddess of grief invites me into Her underworld so often.

But what has helped me continue to feel lush, fertile, and joyful like Inanna, Aphrodite, Yemanya, and Isis is relishing in the gifts and pleasures of my body temple, appreciating how healthy and vibrant I actually am and celebrating all I have and continue to birth. Above all, I have found grace by surrendering to this journey and living as the whole woman and creative, life-giving, flourishing Goddess that I already and truly am.

No matter what part of your life may feel barren, beloved, Isis reminds you that it is okay, natural, and even Divine to have this be. You are a Goddess no matter what has or hasn't come to be for you. You are creative. You are complete. You are Isis.

Like Yemanya, Isis is both the Creatress and the Crone. As Isis proclaims in "The Thunder, Perfect Mind," She is both "the midwife and She who does not bear" and the "solace of (Her) labor pains." Isis is simultaneously the midwife and the mother who strains in Her labor pains. Isis is the Wise Woman who will midwife your dreams into being, providing comfort and healing through the pains of creation. But no matter what you birth or don't, She reminds you to remain content in your own self-containment.

It is worthwhile to note Isis's admission of labor pains, given that the present approach of natural birthing focuses heavily on pain-free and even blissful births, just as much as feminine empowerment messages pose that as women, we can bring forth our dreams solely with ease and joy.

While all women desire a peaceful birthing journey for whatever we are bringing forth, birthing is one of the greatest initiations of our lives. And the initiations that life brings us almost always come with uncertainty, labor, and even pain. The Goddess way is not to fight this, but embrace it. The ease and joy we speak of on the Goddess path does not mean that we won't experience discomfort in our lives. It means that we will accept and ride the waves and surges of our lives, just as we do in labor.

Whether we are birthing a baby or an inspired creation, Isis assures you that laboring is a natural and necessary part of the process. There may be pain and uncertainty. Your patience and faith will be tested. And this is natural. Don't feel like there is something wrong with you or what you are doing. Periods can hurt. Pregnancy can hurt. Labor can hurt. Don't fight the pains, but, like Isis Herself, move through them with surrendered perseverance.

Isis also reminds you that, like Her, you deserve to be supported during any birthing initiation. When Isis gave birth to Horus, She sat alone in the Nile marshes and was agonized by Her labor pains. She squatted down and strained to push Horus out, but to no avail. It wasn't until two Gods came to Her aid and smeared blood (the liquid of life) on Her forehead that She was finally able to birth Horus.

Isis reminds you that even the Goddess of all deities and Divine powers needed support when She struggled to give birth to Her Divine child. So please take the pressure off yourself, beloved. Don't let anyone make you feel like you are less of a woman or Goddess when you, like Isis, are in despair. Instead, allow yourself to be supported like a Queen Goddess, while embracing the natural labor pains of your initiations and creations.

Isis, like Yemanya, is all the cycles of life, death, and renewal that flow through you every moon and during your womanly initiations. She invites you to dance with these sacred rhythms, spiraling through your Maiden-Mother-Crone phases as a whole and empowered Queen.

ISIS AS THE GODDESS OF ABUNDANCE

A Queen is regal and rich, and Isis is here to open you up to receiving your earthly bounty as Pachamama. She is the power within you to manifest material supply through the source of abundance within as She proclaims to Lucius: "I am nature, the parent of things, the Queen of all the elements, the primordial progeny of ages."[31]

She is the primal *shakti* power within you and every woman that can create galaxies. Why ask so little of yourself when you can birth worlds into being, beloved? She is the holy child of the universe that you are. Why settle for so little when you are worthy of all the abundance of heaven and earth?

As Lucius says to Her in his prayer of thanks to Isis: "The hours and seasons return by thy appointment, and the elements reverence thy decree. By thy nod blasts of wind blow, the clouds are nourished, seeds germinate, and blossoms increase."[32]

When you awaken your *shakti* powers, you work with Divine and natural forces to prosper

Isis is the primal **shakti** *power within you and every woman that creates galaxies.*

---

31 Apuleius, *The Metamorphosis, or The Golden Ass, and Philosophical Works of Apuleius*, trans. Thomas Taylor (London: Sold by R. Triphook and T. Rodd, 1822).

32 Ibid.

and flourish. When you claim yourself as a Queen, you wear the crown of self-worth, commanding to be respected, supported, and valued in all your majesty.

Isis as the Goddess of Alchemy

Commanding rightful treatment is essential in order for you to own your Wise Woman gifts as you did with Brigid, given the collective traumas that have held us sorceresses back for so long. Alchemy, magic, spiritual knowledge, and healing are some of Isis's most renowned powers, and She will delight in igniting them within you as Brigid has.

Just as we can awaken our latent spiritual gifts on our own healing journeys, Isis transmuted the lead of Her limitations into the gold of magical abilities and spiritual powers, which She used to protect Her son, Herself, and Her people.

It was during Her desperate and grief-filled search for Osiris's corpse that She transformed Herself into a swallow or kite, becoming a Goddess of shape-shifting and transformation.

It was the second time that She recovered all His dismembered parts that She invented embalming, becoming the patron Goddess of death rites and the afterlife.

It was in Her fervent attempt to resurrect Osiris

that She grew Her glorious wings, becoming a Goddess of freedom and protection.

It was Her ability to revive Osiris through the chanting of spells that made Her the Goddess of *heka* (Kemetic word for magic), *hesi* (sacred chants), ritual, and resurrection.

It was the miraculous conception of Horus during Her tragic, final act of lovemaking with Osiris that turned Her into a Goddess of fertility and one who could change fate.

As a single mother cast out of Her Queendom and living in fear and hiding from Her brother Set, Isis required additional magical power to keep young Horus safe. Her resolve to do so compelled Her to extract the secret name of Her grandfather, the Egyptian sun-God Ra, using the magic and cunning already at Her disposal.

In the myth, Isis created a snake whose venom was mixed with Ra's own saliva, making the otherwise invulnerable God susceptible to its poison. She placed the snake on Ra's daily journey. When Ra was stung, Isis watched quietly as all the other Gods failed in Their attempts to relieve Him.

Finally, Isis offered to help, but claimed that She required His real name in order to work Her magic. As the Egyptians believed that one's real name contained one's true power, it was guarded above all treasures. Reluctantly, Ra eventually relinquished His real name, asking that She never reveal it to anyone else (a promise She upheld).

Once She learned His secret name, Isis kept Her word and used Her magic to save Ra. She was then able to use Her amplified powers for Her true aim, and healed Horus of everything from migraines to a deadly scorpion sting as She raised Him on Her own. Along the way, She became revered as the Mistress of charms and enchantments, Lady of incantations, the Great Goddess who heals, Great Sorceress, and Lady of the flame as She used Her gifts to help fellow deities and humans alike.

Her perseverance and dedication ascended Isis to the status of most powerful of the deities in the knowledge of magic and healing.

Isis as your inner Brigid—your inner alchemist, healer, magician, medicine woman, spellcaster, witch, midwife, and Wise Woman—reminds you that through every tragedy and test you face on your path, you will also cultivate greater wisdom, resilience, and power within you that will elevate you to heights you may otherwise never know.

And with each level you rise to, your own spiritual gifts will expand, which you can use to channel miracles for yourself and others. You become, like Isis, the High Priestess who initiates fellow

> *Through every tragedy and test you face on your path, you will also cultivate greater wisdom, resilience, and power within you that will elevate you to heights you may otherwise never know.*

sisters back into their spiritual strength and magical gifts by living from your own.

ISIS AS THE QUEEN GODDESS OF ALL

As the Queen of the celestials, Supreme of all Divinities, Queen of all elements and realms, light of the Goddesses, and Goddess of All, Isis is all of your Divine Feminine powers. She is the luminescent essence of all the Goddesses fused in you.

And Her journey is one of all women. In going through everything, She becomes the Queen of everything. She faces and transcends all initiations, becoming the rightful ruler of all. She reminds you that while neither us women nor the Goddesses themselves are invulnerable to trauma and tragedy, you can transform the greatest pains of your life into your greatest Sacred Feminine gifts. You can apply them beyond your own life and share them in sacred service and with Divine purpose.

Just as She did with Osiris, when Horus became king of Egypt, Isis continued to lead and serve Her people with grace, wisdom, and love. When Her time came to ascend into the afterlife Herself,

While neither us women nor the Goddesses are invulnerable to trauma and tragedy, you can transform the greatest pains of your life into your greatest Sacred Feminine gifts.

She joined Osiris and ruled as Queen alongside him, but in Her own right and with Her own self-directed roles.

As Her powers and worship continued to expand, She became incorporated into new and existing Goddesses all over the world, attaining Her title as Goddess of Ten Thousand (or Infinite/Endless) Names. What Isis really represents as the omnipresent Goddess, beloved, is your own omnipotent nature as a woman.

When you can own every part of yourself as Divine, you become a powerful leader in the world by way of giving other women permission to claim their sovereignty as well. While you are empowered to become a leader on behalf of any cause you wish, you also don't have to take on any specific worldly role to be a leader. Nor do you need to wait until you feel experienced, credible, or good enough. You lead simply through your own shining example of fully embracing your life lessons and being your true Goddess self.

As you live from your Divine power and inspire fellow women to do the same, you contribute to the resurrection of the Sacred Feminine, the reclamation of the Goddess, and the restoration of sacred sisterhood.

You demonstrate that you don't need any permission outside of yourself to rest in your power to take the lead in your life and to be the all-ruling Queen of your world.

You hold space for us all to shine our light and share our gifts by honoring your own. You inspire us all to rise up as Queens who support and celebrate each other's unique journeys. You become a radiant living vessel for Isis, Goddess of all, to rise again through you and every woman on earth.

It is time now, sister, to wear your crown and take your throne. To sit, like Isis, as the Sovereign Queen in your life and in the world.

Pre-Initiation Preparation:

- Advance prep: if you can, buy yourself a crown, tiara, or garland, as well as a rattle (or simply make your own rattle by adding rice in a sealed container).

- Adorn your altar with flowers, incense, crystals, candles, or anything you feel guided to.

- Wear a fancy dress, one that makes you feel like a queen.

- Adorn yourself with beautiful makeup, jewelry, the crown if you have it, and perfume.

- Use your nicest chair or cover a regular chair with a beautiful cloth.

- Play ancient Egyptian music in the background.

Isis's Initiation:
Taking Your Throne
Ritual Type: Guided Meditation

Sit on your adorned chair in all your regal attire. Close your eyes and chant the ancient Kemetic invocation to Isis, *"Dua Isis"* or *"Dua Ast"* three times (*dua* means "I invoke/praise/give thanks to") as you shake your rattle. Rest your hands on your lap now, still holding the rattle if you wish.

Listen to the music you have chosen for this initiation. Let it move through you, transporting you instantly into the inner realms. See yourself arriving at the doors of a royal temple palace. It is lined with tall, majestic columns inscribed with the wisdom of all the Goddesses.

Announce yourself as:

"I Am (your name), daughter of (your mother's name), granddaughter of (both your grandmothers' names)."

The door opens and you are welcomed in by regal priestesses.

At the throne, you see glorious Isis waiting for you with Her arms and wings outstretched.

She draws you to Her, and now you are right with Her. She wraps you in Her protective wings, and you feel the embrace of the Great Goddess enfold you. Melt into Her as the Queen Mother Goddess holds you with deepest reverence and love.

She says She has been waiting a long time to welcome you back, to appoint you on your rightful seat upon your throne, where you have always belonged.

She calls in all the Divine Feminine aspects of Herself, all aspects of yourself, and they appear as infinite Goddesses—the thirteen other Goddesses you have already met and countless more.

They begin to offer you, Their fellow sister Queen Goddess, Their unique gifts of love.

They bestow upon you the sacred spiral, the endless abyss through which all comes through.

They gift you with the flower of life, which bears the seeds for all of creation.

They gift to you the Divine spark, so that you may transform and transmute what doesn't serve you.

They gift to you the chalice of holy water, so that you may heal and bless all you need to.

They gift to you the sword of truth, so that you may overcome all inner and outer obstacles with fierce grace.

They gift to you a shower of gold, so that abundance may flow forth from your Divine center.

They gift to you the quill of creation, so that you may express your highest inspirations.

They gift to you the lotus flower, so that you may rise above all heartaches and trials.

They gift to you a magical wand, so that you may will your desires into miraculous manifestations.

They gift to you the holy fruit—the red apple—so that you may awaken to the feminine mysteries.

They gift to you the sacred serpent, so that you may unleash your full *shakti* force.

They gift to you the wise owl, so that you may resurrect your spiritual powers.

They gift you with bountiful more blessings. Receive them graciously as you sit in your Queenly worth and value.

In groups, the Goddesses come before you. They are here to bless you. They are here to *be you*.

Isis now invites all Goddesses of the void and sacred silence to merge with you.

Isis invites the Goddesses of the underworld and heaven to merge with you.

Isis invites the Goddesses of feminine wrath and transformation to merge with you.

Isis invites the warrior Goddesses of liberation and empowerment to merge with you.

Isis invites the Goddesses of grace and compassion to merge with you.

Isis invites the Goddesses of Divine love, pleasure, passion, sexuality, and joy to merge with you.

Isis invites the Goddesses of aspiration, inspiration, and self-realization to merge with you.

Isis invites the Goddesses of wisdom, strategy, and action to merge with you.

Isis invites the Goddesses of freedom, integrity, and honor to merge with you.

Isis invites the Maiden-Mother-Crone Triple Goddesses of womb wisdom to merge with you.

Isis invites the Goddesses of abundance, sustenance, and support to merge with you.

Isis invites the Goddesses of healing, miracles, magic, and creativity to merge with you.

Isis invites the Goddesses of the sun, moon, stars, earth, and all of creation to merge with you.

She initiates you once and for all as the Divine Creatress, Priestess, Warrioress, Maiden, Mother, Crone, Lover, Muse, Life-giver, Destroyer, Transformer, Transmuter, Initiator, Leader, Wild Woman, Huntress, Oracle, Seer, Sorceress, Magician, Alchemist, Miracle Worker, Witch, Midwife, Healer, Sustainer, Nourisher, Enchantress, Savioress, Protectress, and Empress.

She places Her crown upon your head and initiates you as the Sovereign Queen Goddess of all that you are. She appoints royal councils and priestesses to serve and support you as you commit to serving and leading on your Divine path.

Seated regally on your throne, you now radiate out all your Sacred Feminine powers from the Goddesses that have merged within you, the Goddesses that you are. Behold as your entire Queendom and all those in it are blessed and uplifted as you do. See now your Goddess essence radiate out in blessing to all.

As you bless all beings everywhere, Isis spreads Her wings again, and showers you with blessings, which pour forth as shimmering *ankhs* (Her sacred symbol of life, drawn as the circle-headed cross).

Isis shares with you a loving message to empower you to transmit this initiation as Queen into your earthly life. Receive Her guidance.

Isis now merges Her holy self with you. Her wings become your wings. Her powers become your powers. She is you. You are Her. She is the Goddess. You are the Goddess.

Come back now, beloved. Slowly, gently. Heart open and head held high. To live as Queen in all of your lives.

POST-INITIATION SELF-CARE:

- Seal in this ritual by shaking Her rattle as you dance in sacred celebration.

- Continue to spend your day in your regal attire.

- Ground this final initiation with Goddess rituals: walking barefoot on the earth, bathing in sea salt water, eating a decadent meal—whatever you feel guided to.

- Write down the next inspired steps you will take to assume your leadership and sovereign power.

- Celebrate the completion of your journey through intuitively guided ceremony: prayer, meditation,

a day at the spa or in nature, or a champagne toast
to yourself!

- Continue to honor your Goddess nature every
  day, for all the Goddesses live through you now.

AFFIRMING ISIS:

I am the Sacred Mistress.
I am the High Priestess.
I am the Heavenly Creatress.
I am the Dark Destructress.
I am the Fearless Warrioress.
I am the Swift Savioress.
I am the Holy Loveress.
I am the Magical Sorceress.
I am the Fierce Protectress.
I am the Wild Huntress.
I am the Intoxicating Enchantress.
I am the Sovereign Queen and Empress.

I am the One and All Goddess.

I Am Isis.

Goddess Isis

Origin: Egyptian

Also Called: Auset, Aset, Ast, Est, Iset

Name Meanings: Throne, Queen, Mother of all Gods and Goddesses, One and All Goddess, Goddess of Ten Thousand Names, Great Goddess

Attributes:

- Goddess of all
- Magic
- Alchemy
- Healing
- Manifesting
- Love
- Royalty
- Mourning
- Queen of heaven
- Queen of the under-world

- Resurrection
- Renewal
- Afterlife
- Ritual
- All elements and cosmos
- Creation
- Transformation
- Initiation
- Civilization
- Law and justice

- Commerce
- Success
- Language
- Protection
- Sacred mysteries
- Dreams and goals
- Prophesy
- High Priestess
- Sacred chants
- Perseverance
- Courage
- Sacred sexuality
- Karmic/past-life healing
- Miracles

- Marriage
- Motherhood
- Leadership
- Fertility
- Abundance
- Spring
- Beauty
- Feminine empowerment
- Women's wisdom
- Changing fate/fortune
- Ascension
- Higher/spiritual perception
- Self-actualization

Sacred Symbols:

- Throne
- Crown (sun disk in the center of cow horns)
- Wings
- Long sheath dress

- Breastfeeding mother
- Milk
- Blood
- *Ankh* (cross with loop/oval head)

- *Tyet* (sacred knot symbol/amulet)
- *Menat* necklace
- *Sistrum* (rattle)
- Sirius (Sopdet)
- Lotus flower
- Sycamore tree
- Papyrus
- Sun and moon
- The Nile
- Hieroglyphics
- Perfume bottles
- Altar
- Kite or swallow
- Vulture
- Scorpion
- Cow

Chakras: All seven (root, sacral, solar plexus, heart, throat, third eye, and crown)

Elements: All (water, air, earth, fire, and ether)

Essential Oils:

- Frankincense
- Sandalwood
- Lotus
- Jasmine
- Cedarwood
- Rose
- Patchouli
- Cinnamon
- Eucalyptus
- Lavender
- Fennel
- Geranium
- Vetiver
- Myrrh

- Fig

Colors:

- Gold
- Silver
- Blue
- Red

Crystals:

- Lapis lazuli
- Red jasper
- Clear quartz
- Carnelian
- Moonstone
- Apache tear
- Obsidian

Archetype in Balance:

- Empowered
- Whole
- Practices self-love and acceptance
- Is always willing to grow
- Takes responsibility for one's healing
- Dedicated to serving others
- Allows one to be supported
- Loyal
- Decisive
- Benevolent
- Generous
- Charismatic
- Fair/just
- Dedicated to one's purpose
- Hones and expresses one's talents

- Shares one's gifts with confidence

- Has a deep and rich spiritual life

- Is the authority in one's life

- Leads and inspires others with grace

- Protects what one values and cherishes

- Embraces change and transformation

- Values spiritual and earthly life equally

- Treats oneself with care and respect

- Is compassionate with oneself and others

- Gets help when one needs it

- Harnesses one's spiritual gifts

- Co-creates the life one desires and deserves with inspired action

- Lives a healthy lifestyle

- Is resourceful and self-sufficient

- Embraces and honors all of oneself

- Has a supportive tribe

- Seeks and intends everyone's highest good

- Loves being a woman

- Appreciates one's feminine gifts

- Is the Queen of one's life

Archetype out of Balance:

- Has difficulty receiving intuitive guidance

- Doesn't trust and follow inner guidance

- Stagnant

- Uninspired
- Gives power away
- Insecure
- Confused
- Lacks focus
- Aggressive
- Martyr
- Victim
- Tries to rescue others
- Has spiritual ego
- Ungrounded
- Can isolate self
- Projects on others

- Doesn't take responsibility for personal wounds
- Lacks self-awareness
- Resists pain and growth
- Hides spiritual side out of fear of judgment or condemnation
- Can have social anxiety
- Can misuse spiritual power
- Manipulative
- Cunning
- Stubborn
- Power-hungry

Creating Balance:

- Maintain your own identity in relationships.
- Empower rather than enable others.

- Trust that everyone is capable of learning their own lessons.
- Respect each person's unique spiritual journey and life path.

- Cultivate your power from within, from your Sovereign nature.

- Use your power consciously and wisely.

- Trust and follow your intuition.

- Prioritize sacred self-care.

- Ask for your needs to be met.

- Assert your boundaries with graceful firmness.

- Get further training to awaken your spiritual gifts.

- Value your time and talents; charge a fair fee for sharing your gifts (or require an energy exchange).

- Consider other's advice, but make your own decisions in the end.

- Look for the lesson in life challenges.

- Create and tend to an altar for your spiritual practices.

- Allow yourself to shine like the star Sirius in the midnight sky.

- Explore past life work to heal karmic patterns and awaken your ancient knowledge and gifts.

- Command rather than demand respect.

- Respect yourself and others.

- Stay true to your purpose and dreams.

- Celebrate your good with others.

- Celebrate others' success.

- Collaborate with others.

- Practice self-love and compassion.

- Invest in the best quality products you can afford.

- Treat yourself to luxurious experiences within your means.

- Make the mundane sacred through ritual and ceremony.

- Use mantras and sacred words, prayers, chants, affirmations, and spells for healing and manifesting.

- Tend to what you love and value.

- Forgive and move forward.

- Hold space for yourself and others.

- Create sacred sisterhood by connecting with and supporting like-minded women

and allow yourself to be supported in turn.

- Attend or host spiritual gatherings, especially women's circles.

- Know that you lead and serve best by being your fullest, truest self.

- Manifest your dreams with spiritual tools (visualization, meditation, prayer, mantras, crystals) and inspired strategic action.

- Embrace challenges as initiations into a higher level of ascension into your power, wisdom, and sovereignty.

Associated Goddesses: All Goddesses, but most specifically:

- Hathor (Egyptian)

- Maat (Egyptian)

- Sekhmet (Egyptian)

- Ishtar (Mesopotamian)

- Aphrodite (Greek)

- Athena (Greek)

- Hecate (Greek)

- Demeter (Greek)

- Hera (Greek)

- Hestia (Greek)

- Artemis (Greek)

- Devi (the Indian/ Hindu All-Goddess)

- Astarte (Middle Eastern)

- Mother Mary (Christian)

- Mary Magdalene (Christian)

- Brigid (Celtic)

- Sophia (Gnostic)

- Kuan Yin (Chinese)

- Tara (Tibetan)

- Yemanya (Yoruba)

- Oshun (Yoruba)

- Eagle Woman (Aztec)

- Inanna and Ereshki-gal (Sumerian)

Prayer/Invocation:

Dua Ast! *Beloved Isis, as Goddess of All within me, thank you for empowering me to sit on the throne of my life as its Sovereign Queen. Help me to wear my crown and own my authority with regal grace.*

Help me to embrace the trials of my life with courage and faith, keeping only the lessons and growth they come to offer. Make me resilient like you so that I may always persevere. I open myself to ascending to the highest heights my soul can reach. I offer myself to be of the greatest service on this earth. Make me a vessel for Divine love, healing, magic, and miracles. Let me recall and re-awaken my Divine Feminine spiritual gifts and use them with reverence for the highest good of all.

Let me lead and inspire as you did. Help me trust and honor my path and gifts and share them wisely and lovingly. Let me be supported as you yourself were. Let me know myself as the All-Goddess that you are, that I am.

Let me spread my wings and soar high like you. Let me love and be loved deeply and completely as you. Let me be all that I am and came here to be, one with you as you are with me. Dua Ast. Dua Ast. Dua Ast. So be it. So it is.

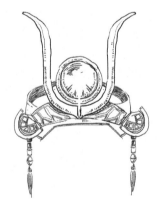

AFTERWORD:

BEING A FLOURISHING GODDESS

Beloved, here you are! My deepest bows of love to you as you celebrate the completion of this journey.

It has been my deepest honor and privilege to serve you through this heart-offering. I pray with all of my heart that you have felt mine and the Goddesses' love and support with you in every word, in every gateway, in every moment.

I hope you will acknowledge and celebrate yourself for your commitment to your own transformation and flourishing by embarking on this journey. You have come so far indeed.

You started with nothing with Sige. And you ended with everything with Isis.

You have met and awakened the Goddesses in all realms and through all elements:

The pregnant emptiness of the ethers with Sige.

The dark depths of the underworld with Inanna and Ereshkigal.

The lava fires of transformation with Pele.

The swirling abyss of timelessness with Kali.

The gentle lotus and holy waters with Kuan Yin.

The passionate waves of the sea with Aphrodite.

The heavenly heights of the stars with Tara.

The clear, crisp air of the Parthenon with Athena.

The wild winds of Lilith's wings.

The light of the moon and rhythm of the ocean with Yemanya.

The bountiful blessings of the earth with Pachamama.

The spark of the alchemical flame with Brigid.

The Queendom of all domains with Isis.

Through each initiation, you have also worked through all your *chakras* and your mental, emotional, physical, spiritual, and energetic bodies.

In resurrecting and embracing all of yourself, you have reclaimed your full Goddess self. This doesn't mean that you will or must always feel all of these Goddesses' powers activated through you in perfect balance. I hope you have rather uncovered that you have the power to invoke and cultivate each one as best serves you on your own journey, beloved.

> *In resurrecting and embracing all of yourself, you have reclaimed your full Goddess self.*

Sometimes you may need the courage of the Warrioress, and sometimes you may need the medicine of the healer. Sometimes you may need the passion of the lover, and sometimes the ferocity of the transformer. Whatever needs and desires arise for you, I hope you now feel empowered to honor them with the Sacred Feminine gifts you have reclaimed.

It is time to now take everything you have learned and received through this journey and activate it in your life with joy, inspiration, and empowerment. And the way is open for you to continue to awaken and hone your countless Goddess gifts. Own and share all the gifts you have ignited and continue to cultivate them as you feel guided.

Let your own reclamation of the Goddess serve as a shining example to fellow sisters and brothers to recover their own Divine nature.

Join and rally fellow women to awaken their own Sacred Feminine power, so that together we may rise again as the Goddesses we truly are and bring back the Goddess in Her full glory through us.

It is time, sister.

You are ready. And we are ready for you.

May you know yourself as the Goddess you are now and always will be and flourish in all ways.

So be it.

So it is.

And blessed be.

ABOUT THE AUTHOR

Syma Kharal is an international Sacred Feminine and spiritual coach, healer, speaker, yoga teacher, and #1 Amazon best-selling author. She holds an honors degree with distinction in psychology and a certificate in counseling from the University of Toronto, and is a certified Reiki Master, Yoga and Meditation teacher, Spirit Guide, and Akashic Records coach.

Syma is dedicated to empowering soulful women

heal their deepest wounds, manifest their boldest dreams, and flourish in every way.

Syma immersed herself in the healing arts at the age of fourteen to overcome the deeply damaging effects of extensive abuse and trauma. In addition to healing herself, her intensive spiritual work led her to co-create a life she never dreamt possible: leaving a toxic corporate career to follow her calling, manifesting and marrying her soulmate, transforming women's lives through her heart's work, and traveling the world with her beloved husband.

She loves nothing more than supporting fellow sisters to do the same—to transcend disempowering patterns, reclaim their full feminine power, and step fully into the Goddesses they truly are.

Receive Syma's free, "Awaken Your Inner Goddesses" guided meditation MP3 at:
FlourishingGoddess.com

Connect with her on:

Facebook: facebook.com/FlourishingGoddess
Instagram: instagram.com/FlourishingGoddess
YouTube: youtube.com/FlourishingGoddessTV

SYMA AT THE CHALICE WELL IN GLASTONBURY,
ENGLAND, 2016, WHERE THIS BOOK WAS REVEALED.

BIBLIOGRAPHY

Angier, Natalie. *Woman: An Intimate Geography*. New York: Mariner, 2014.

Apuleius. *The Metamorphosis, or The Golden Ass, and Philosophical Works of Apuleius*. Translated by Thomas Taylor. London: Sold by R. Triphook and T. Rodd, 1822.

Armour, Robert A. *Gods and Myths of Ancient Egypt*. Cairo: American University in Cairo, 2002.

Ashley-Farrand, Thomas. *Shakti Mantras: Tapping into the Great Goddess Energy Within*. New York: Ballantine, 2003.

"Avalokiteshvara." In *Encyclopedia Britannica*. Article published May 27, 2015. https://global.britannica.com/topic/Avalokiteshvara

Bachofen, Johann Jacob. "Mother Right: An investigation of religious and juridical character of matriarchy in the ancient world." In *Myth, Religion and Mother Right*. London: Routledge and Kegan Paul, 1967.

Ball, Pamela J. *Natural Magic: Spells, Enchantments & Self-Development*. London: Arcturus, 2010.

Beck, Martha. *Finding Your Own North Star: Claiming The Life You Were Meant To Live*. New York: Crown Publishers, 2001.

Black, J.A., G. Cunningham, E. Fluckiger-Hawker, E. Robson, and G. Zólyomi. *The Electronic Text Corpus of Sumerian Literature*. Oxford, 1998. http://etcsl.orient.ox.ac.uk.

Bolen, Jean Shinoda. *Goddesses in Every Woman: Powerful Archetypes in Women's Lives*. San Francisco: Harper Perennial, 1984.

Bradley, Marion Zimmer. *The Mists of Avalon*. New York: Ballantine Pub. Group, 2000.

Bronznick, Norman. "The Alphabet of ben Sira." In *Rabbinic Fantasies: Imaginative Narratives from Classical Hebrew Literature*. Edited by David Stern and Mark Jay Mirsky. Philadelphia: Jewish Publication Society, 1990.

Budge, Wallis E.A. *The Book of the Dead*. Based on the *Papyrus of Ani* in possession of the British Museum. London: British Museum Order of Trustees, 1895.

Campbell, Joseph. *Goddesses: Mysteries of the Feminine Divine*. Edited by Safron Rossi. Novato: Joseph Campbell Foundation, 2013.

———. *The Power of Myth*. With Bill Moyers. Edited by Betty Sue Flowers. New York: Doubleday, 1998.

Canson, Patricia E. "Yemonja." In *Encyclopedia Britannica*. Article published August 15, 2014. https://www.britannica.com/topic/Yemonja

Carpenter, Thomas H. *Art and Myth in Ancient Greece*. London: Thames and Hudson, 2006.

Cartwright, Mark. "Kali." In *Ancient History Encyclopedia*. Article published June 21, 2013. https://www.ancient.eu/Kali/

Cotterell, Arthur. *The Encyclopedia of Mythology: Norse, Greek & Roman, Celtic*. London: Hermes House, 2011.

The Dalai Lama, and Renuka Singh. *The Path to Tranquility: Daily Wisdom*. New York: Penguin Books, 2002.

Diamant, Anita. *The Red Tent.* New York: A Wyatt Book for St. Martin's Press, 1997.

Dixon-Kennedy, Mike. *Celtic Myth & Legend: An A-Z of People and Places.* London: Blandford, 1997.

Dyer, Wayne W. *Manifest Your Destiny: The Nine Spiritual Principles for Getting Everything You Want.* New York: HarperCollins, 1999.

Eden, Donna. *Energy Medicine for Women.* With David Feinstein. London: Piatkus, 2009.

Ehrenreich, Barbara, and Deirdre English. *Witches, Midwives, & Nurses: A History of Women Healers.* New York: The Feminist Press, 1973.

Farrar, Janet, and Stewart Farrar. *A Witches Bible Compleat.* New York: Magickal Childe, 1986.

Farrer-Halls, Gill. *The Aromatherapy Bible: The Definitive Guide to Using Essential Oils.* Alresford: Godsfield, 2009.

Frawley, David. *Tantric Yoga and the Wisdom Goddesses: Spiritual Secrets of Ayurveda.* Delhi: Motilala Banarsidass, 2005.

Gimbutas, Marija. *The Language of the Goddess*. London: Thames & Hudson, 2006.

———. *The Living Goddesses*. Edited by Miriam Robbins Dexter. Berkeley: University of California, 2005.

Grant, Frederick C. *The Aretalogy of Isis from Hellenistic Religions: The Age of Syncretism*. New York: Liberal Arts Press, 1953.

Gray, Miranda. *Red Moon: Understanding and Using the Creative, Sexual and Spiritual Gifts of the Menstrual Cycle*. Shaftesbury: Dancing Eve, 2009.

Greenwood, Susan. *Witchcraft: A History: The Study of Magic and Necromancy Through the Ages*. London: Lorenz, 2013.

Hay, Louise L. *You can Heal Your Life*. Santa Monica, CA : Hay House Inc., 1987.

Jennings, Sue. *Goddesses: Ancient Wisdom for Times of Change from over 70 Goddesses*. Carlsbad, CA: Hay House, 2005.

Katz, Steven T. *The Holocaust in Historical Context*. Volume 1, *The Holocaust and Mass Death before the Modern Age*. Oxford University Press, 1995.

Keim, Joni, and Ruah Bull. *Daily Aromatherapy: Transforming the Seasons of Your Life with Essential Oils.* Berkeley: North Atlantic, 2008.

Kempton, Sally. *Awakening Shakti: The Transformative Power of the Goddesses of Yoga.* Boulder: Sounds True Inc., 2013.

Levack, Brian P. *The Witch-Hunt in Early Modern Europe.* London: Routledge, Taylor & Francis Group, 2016.

Loar, Julie. *Goddesses for Every Day: Exploring the Wisdom & Power of the Divine Feminine around the World.* Novato: New World Library, 2011.

MacRae, George W. "The Thunder, Perfect Mind." In *Nag Hammadi.* Codex VI, *Tractate 2: Protocol of the Fifth Colloquy* (1973). The Center for Hermeneutical Studies in Hellenistic and Modern Culture, 1975.

Mark, Joshua J. "Inanna." In *Ancient History Encyclopedia.* Article published October 15, 2010. https://www.ancient.eu/Inanna/

Martin, Wilson. *In Praise of Tara: Songs to the Saviouress.* Somerville: Wisdom Publications, 1992.

McConnel, Jen. *Goddess Spells for Busy Girls: Get Rich, Get Happy, Get Lucky*. San Francisco: Weiser, 2014.

Monaghan, Patricia. *The Goddess Path: Myths, Invocations & Rituals*. St. Paul, MN: Llewellyn, 1999.

Myss, Caroline. *Anatomy of the Spirit: The Seven Stages of Power and Healing*. London: Bantam Books, 1997.

Naydler, Jeremy. *Temple of the Cosmos: The Ancient Egyptian Experience of the Sacred*. Rochester: Inner Traditions, 1996.

New American Standard Bible. California: Foundation Publications, 2015.

Northrup, Christiane. *Goddesses Never Age: The Secret Prescription for Radiance, Vitality, and Well-Being*. Carlsbad, CA: Hay House, Inc., 2015.

———. *Mother-daughter Wisdom: Creating a Legacy of Physical And Emotional Health*. New York: Bantam Books, 2005.

Owen, Lara. *Her Blood Is Gold: Awakening to the Wisdom of Menstruation*. Dorset: Archive, 2008.

Plutarch. *Moralia, Volume V: Isis and Osiris. The E at Delphi. The Oracles at Delphi No Longer Given in Verse. The Obsolescence of Oracles.* Translated by Frank Cole Babbitt. Loeb Classical Library edition, 1936.

Queen Afua. *Sacred Woman: A Guide to Healing the Feminine Body, Mind, and Spirit.* New York: One World, 2001.

Regardie, Israel. *The Middle Pillar: The Balance Between Mind and Magic.* Saint Paul, MN: Llewellyn Publications, 1987.

Rose, Sharron. *The Path of the Priestess: A Guidebook for Awakening the Divine Feminine.* Inner Traditions, 2002.

Schweizer, Andreas. *The Sungod's Journey through the Netherworld: Reading the Ancient Egyptian Amduat.* Edited by David Lorton. Ithaca: Cornell University, 2010.

Sjoo, Monica, and Barbara Mor. *The Great Cosmic Mother: Rediscovering the Religion of the Earth.* San Francisco: HarperOne, an Imprint of HarperCollins Publishers, 2012.

Skye, Michelle. *Goddess Alive! Inviting Celtic & Norse Goddesses into Your Life.* Woodbury, MN: Llewellyn Publications, 2007.

Starhawk. *The Spiral Dance: A Rebirth of the Ancient Religion of the Great Goddess.* New York: HarperCollins Publishers, 1979.

Stassinopoulos, Agapi. *Conversations with the Goddesses: Revealing the Divine Power Within You.* New York: Stewart, Tabori & Chang, 1999.

Stern, David, ed., and Mark Jay Mirsky, ed. *Rabbinic Fantasies: Imaginative Narratives from Classical Hebrew Literature.* Yale Judaica Series. Philadelphia, Jewish Publication Society, 1990.

Stone, Merlin. *When God Was a Woman.* Orlando: Harcourt, 2014.

Telesco, Patricia. *365 Goddess: A Daily Guide to the Magic and Inspiration of the Goddess.* New York: HarperCollins Publishers, 1998.

Valiente, Doreen. "The Charge Of The Goddess." The Official Doreen Valiente Website. http://www.doreenvaliente.com/Doreen-Valiente-Doreen_Valiente_Poetry-11.php

Vanderlip, Vera Fredericka. *The Four Greek Hymns of Isidorus and the Cult of Isis.* Toronto: A. M. Hakkert, Ltd., 1972.

Vanzant, Iyanla. *Forgiveness: 21 Days to Forgive Everyone for Everything*. Carlsbad, California: Smiley Books, Distributed by Hay House, Inc., 2013.

Virtue, Doreen. *Archangels & Ascended Masters: A Guide to Working and Healing with Divinities and Deities*. Carlsbad, CA: Hay House Inc., 2009.

Vitti, Alisa. *WomanCode: Perfect Your Cycle, Amplify Your Fertility, Supercharge Your Sex Drive, and Become a Power Source*. New York: HarperOne, 2014.

Wauters, Ambika. *The Complete Guide to Chakras: Unleash the Positive Power Within*. Hauppauge, NY: Barron's, 2010.

Wilkinson, Richard H. *The Complete Gods and Goddesses of Ancient Egypt*. London: Thames & Hudson, 2005.

Wolkstein, Diane, and Samuel Noah Kramer. *Inanna, Queen of Heaven and Earth: Her Stories and Hymns from Sumer*. New York: Harper & Row, 2004.

"Yemaya." In *God Checker*. Edited by Peter J. Allen and Chas Saunders. Article last updated April 19, 2013. http://www.godchecker.com/pantheon/african-mythology.php?deity=YEMAYA

Yogananda. *The Essence of Self-Realization: The Wisdom of Paramhansa Yogananda*. Recorded and compiled by Swami Kriyananda. Nevada City, CA: Crystal Clarity, 1990.

Zabel, Gary, *Case Study: The European Witch-Hunts, C. 1450-1750 and Witch-Hunts Today*. Massachusetts: University of Massachusetts Boston, 1999.